Love the Sin

SEXUAL CULTURES: New Directions from the Center for
Lesbian and Gay Studies
General Editors: José Esteban Muñoz and Ann Pellegrini

Times Square Red, Times Square Blue
Samuel R. Delany

Private Affairs: *Critical Ventures in the Culture of Social Relations*
Phillip Brian Harper

In Your Face: *9 Sexual Studies*
Mandy Merck

Tropics of Desire: *Interventions from Queer Latino America*
José Quiroga

Murdering Masculinities: *Fantasies of Gender and Violence*
in the American Crime Novel
Greg Forter

Our Monica, Ourselves: *The Clinton Affair and the National Interest*
Edited by Lauren Berlant and Lisa Duggan

Black Gay Man: *Essays*
Robert Reid-Pharr *Foreword by Samuel R. Delany*

Passing: *Identity and Interpretation in Sexuality, Race, and Religion*
Edited by María Carla Sánchez and Linda Schlossberg

The Queerest Art: *Essays on Lesbian and Gay Theater*
Edited by Alisa Solomon and Framji Minwalla

Queer Globalizations: *Citizenship and the Afterlife of Colonialism*
Edited by Arnaldo Cruz-Malavé and Martin F. Manalansan IV

Queer *Latinidad*: *Identity Practices, Discursive Spaces*
Juana María Rodríguez

Love the Sin: *Sexual Regulation and the Limits of Religious Tolerance*
Janet R. Jakobsen and Ann Pellegrini

Love the Sin

Sexual Regulation and the Limits
of Religious Tolerance

JANET R. JAKOBSEN AND ANN PELLEGRINI

NEW YORK UNIVERSITY PRESS

New York and London

NEW YORK UNIVERSITY PRESS
New York and London

© 2003 by New York University

Library of Congress Cataloging-in-Publication Data
Jakobsen, Janet R., 1960–
Love the Sin : sexual regulation and the limits
of religious tolerance / Janet R. Jakobsen and Ann Pellegrini.
p. cm. — (Sexual cultures)
Includes bibliographical references and index.
ISBN 0-8147-4264-5 (alk. paper)
1. Homosexuality—Religious aspects—Christianity.
2. Gay rights—Religious aspects—Christianity.
3. Homosexuality—Government policy—United States.
4. Gay rights—United States.   I. Pellegrini, Ann, 1964–
II. Title.   III. Series.
BR115.H6 J34 2003
291.1'7835766'0973—dc21   2002012273

New York University Press books are printed on acid-free paper,
and their binding materials are chosen for strength and durability.

Manufactured in the United States of America

10 9 8 7 6 5 4 3 2 1

For those we love,
in the fullness and complexity of all that means.

Contents

Acknowledgments   ix

Introduction: Why Religion, Why Sex?   1

1   **Getting Religion**   19

2   **What's Wrong with Tolerance?**   45

3   **Not Born That Way**   75

4   **The Free Exercise of Sex**   103

5   **Valuing Sex**   127

Conclusion: Open Endings, Dreaming America   149

Notes   153

Index   169

About the Authors   175

Acknowledgments

This book marks a different kind of writing for both of us. Not only is it collaborative, when collaborative articles and books in the humanities are a rarity (especially in comparison to the sciences and social sciences), but it also represents something of a departure from the densely footnoted work we have produced in our more traditionally academic writing. We have not, however, left our scholarly personae (or footnotes) behind altogether. Rather, we hope in these pages to connect the questions we have asked, both individually and together, in sometimes arcane academic circles to ongoing public debates about religious and sexual freedom in the United States.

In this book, we argue for the production of new values through various forms of intimacy. These intimacies and the values they enable do not come from nowhere, but emerge in part out of social movements. We would even say that social movements, such as the African American civil rights movement, and women's and gay liberation, are among the conditions of possibility for the new intimacies and values championed in these pages. We accordingly want to begin by thanking those social movements that have taught us just how much can come out of thinking and working together toward a different kind of future.

This book is the product, then, not just of the many conversations and debates between the two of us, but also of the many generous contributions of colleagues, friends, interlocutors, and opponents along the way. We lay out their contributions in some detail here so as to acknowledge the breadth of activity—and hence the depth of our gratitude—that is encapsulated in the term "collaborative writing."

Our own conversations began long before we undertook the actual writing of this book. The ideas that became *Love the Sin* were first articulated in a panel that we organized in 1994 for the annual meeting of the American Academy of Religion. That panel, which presented a feminist, queer, and antiracist critique of the right-wing video *Gay Rights, Special Rights,* helped us to understand some of the limits of the arguments that were being promoted not just by the political Right, but also by proponents of gay rights. With the help of our copanelists—both new friends and longtime mentors—Renee Hill, Mary Hunt, and Beverly Wildung Harrison, we came to see that public discussion of gay rights needed to shift. It was at this panel that Janet first began the critique of tolerance that formed the kernel of what is now chapter 2 and Ann first proposed the connection between religious freedom and sexual freedom that is at the heart of chapter 3.

Since that time, a number of proponents (some of whom we have been in direct conversation with, and some not) across the political spectrum have proposed an analogy between the disestablishment of religion and the disestablishment of sexuality, while others have proposed connections between religious liberty or free exercise and gay rights. We welcome this growing chorus of voices, which includes Rebecca Alpert, Lisa Duggan, David A. J. Richards, Michael W. McConnell, Andrew Koppelman, Kathleen M. Sands, and Andrew Sullivan. (The various ends to which this diverse group of thinkers puts their arguments indicate that the analogy does not, in and of itself, make any one political case.)

Our own process of writing together came through the opportunity to present a joint paper at the conference "One Nation under God?" held at the Humanities Center at Harvard University in 1997. We are deeply grateful to Marjorie Garber and Rebecca Walkowitz, who organized this conference, for the stimulating environment of those few days and for sparking a process that for us has been both pleasurable and productive.

Over the course of the ensuing years, we have presented parts of the book in various venues, and we would like to acknowledge the contributions of those who listened to, read, and most importantly, engaged with these arguments as they were formed. We presented materials from this book side by side on a panel at the

December 1999 annual meeting of the Modern Language Association. That panel—on the subject "Why Religion? Why Now?"—was organized by the Division for Gay Studies in Language and Literature, and we especially want to thank our fellow panelists Henry Abelove, José Esteban Muñoz, and Geeta Patel.

Janet presented parts of chapter 2 at the Humanities Center at Harvard in 1998, while a fellow at the Center for the Study of Values and Public Life at Harvard Divinity School. She also received comments from the faculty seminar in Women's Studies at the University of Arizona, a talk organized by Donna Smith at Emory University, and one organized by Gwendolyn Dean at Cornell University. The opportunity to publish a short rendition in *Sojourner: The Women's Forum,* a longtime activist publication of the type that makes certain publics possible, was particularly helpful. We were once again able to present our ideas about tolerance together at Barnard College in February 1999, and we thank then–acting director of the Center for Research on Women, Angela Zito, for inviting us to do so.

Ann presented pieces of chapter 3 to a number of audiences, including New York University, where she participated in a panel discussion on homosexuality, the Bible, and public policy in 1998; Wesleyan University's Center for the Humanities; the Ninth Annual Women and Society Conference, held at Marist College; the University Program in Cultural Studies at the University of North Carolina at Chapel Hill; a colloquium in gender theories hosted by the Department of English at Boston College; and Grinnell College, where she was invited to help launch Queer Pride Week in April 2000. There are so many people to thank for these opportunities, among them: Judith Farquhar, Ariel Herrera, JoAnne Myers, Frances Restuccia, Tyler Roberts, Kathleen Roberts Skerrett, Min Song, and Elizabeth Traub. Ann also wants to acknowledge the Department of Women's Studies at Barnard College and the Department of Drama at the University of California, Irvine, both of which provided research support for the completion of this project.

We owe a special debt to the Queer Faculty Group at New York University. They were kind enough to read an early version of chapter 1 during a year when the group was organized by José Esteban Muñoz and Lisa Duggan and, in 2001, to read a version of chapter 4 once Carolyn Dinshaw had taken up leadership of the Center for the Study of Gender and Sexuality. Rob Corber, another organizer of the group that year, re-presented our ideas to us in the succinct formulation that "disestablishment is not the same as secularism." The work of organizing such groups is rarely given credit, and yet without it there would be no such thing as intellectual life. This group has over the years provided an extremely nurturing environment, offering us the chance to read and engage the inspiring and thought-provoking work of our colleagues, including Ed Cohen, Douglas Crimp, Ann Cvetkovich, Florence Dure, David Eng, Licia Fiol-Matta, Elizabeth Freeman, Phillip Brian Harper, Martin Manalansan, Anna McCarthy, Gus Stadler, and Patty White. Katherine Franke at the Columbia University Law School Center for the Study of Law and Culture organized a helpful conversation, which ended up taking place over a lovely dinner, that included David Eng and Renée Römkens. Teemu Ruskola also provided sage legal counsel (often also over lovely dinners). We also received extremely helpful comments from an audience at the New School University, where we had the opportunity to present an early version of chapter 4.

Another panel at the American Academy of Religion in 1997 on the work of David M. Halperin with David, Daniel Boyarin, and Elizabeth Clarke provided some crucial seeds for chapter 5. This chapter also owes much to Janet's collaboration with Elizabeth Lapovsky Kennedy on another project, "Sex and Freedom." A paper with that title was first presented at a wonderful seminar on "Sexuality and the State," which was organized at the International Center for the Sociology of Law in Oñati, Spain, by Elizabeth Bernstein and Laurie Schaffner. The effort to connect sex and freedom has become part of a larger project on creating paradigm shifts in public debates on feminist sexuality, and we're grateful to leadership from Paola Bacchetta, Lauren Berlant, Amber Hollibaugh, and Liz Kennedy.

We have been extraordinarily fortunate to work with Eric Zinner at NYU Press. He not only encouraged us at every stage of this project but even came up with the book's title. We cannot begin to thank Eric enough for his good humor, intellectual imagination, and editorial patience. Others at NYU Press also made our lives a lot easier, especially Emily Park, who answered all our last-minute questions seconds before we asked them, or so it seemed. For the beautiful image that graces this book's cover, we want to thank the artist Kathleen Gilje as well as Rodney Hill of Gorney Bravin + Lee Gallery and Paul B. Franklin, who sent us down to Gorney Bravin + Lee in the first place.

Finally, we must acknowledge the daily engagement and support from our friends, colleagues, and lovers, who make work and love possible. Many of those we have named above have contributed in multiple ways to our lives. Some others who have contributed importantly to the possibility of this book include Karen Anderson, Laura Berry, Mark Bogosian, Elizabeth Castelli, Adam Christian, Bill Handley, Alice Jardine, Miranda Joseph, Natalie Kampen, Juliana Kubala, Laura Levitt, Molly McGarry, Afsaneh Najmabadi, Linda Nicholson, Linda Norton, Rebecca Schneider, Juliet Schor, Beverly Seckinger, Randall Styers, and David Harrington Watt. We would particularly like to thank Elizabeth Budnitz and David Hopson for making work fun, and we are eternally indebted to the research assistance of Irene Xanthoudakis. During the final stages of editing, Robin Weigert was a heart-stretching gadfly, Linda Schlossberg provided perfectly balanced editorial incisions (as well as fiercely enduring friendship), and Henry Abelove offered crucial technical assistance. Christina Crosby and her lovely companion, Babe, make all things possible. And, of course, we remain indebted to all those untold persons who have had the courage to love the sinner and the sin.

Introduction

Why Religion, Why Sex?

Love the Sinner. Hate the Sin. This familiar catch-phrase seems to be the guide for thinking about a number of contemporary moral issues, particularly those having to do with sex. In debates over homosexuality, reproductive rights, and teen pregnancy and welfare policy, the distinction between sin and sinner, act and person, seems to provide a middle ground, a compromise in which all are welcomed to the table, no one has to change deeply felt moral convictions, and, better still, no one gets hurt. But do things really work this way?

Love the sinner, hate the sin means that when Christians like Rev. Jerry Falwell or media personalities like Dr. Laura denounce homosexuality, they are not being hateful. They are simply taking a moral stand about a particular act or set of acts. In practice, however, love the sinner, hate the sin allows people to take positions that are punitive toward their fellow citizens, while at the same time experiencing themselves as being not simply ethical, but compassionate and even tolerant of difference.

Professions of tolerance mixed with stern moral judgments have become routine in American political life. For example, in a television interview in the summer of 1998, then–senate majority leader Trent Lott addressed the question of homosexuality and gay rights. Asked whether homosexuality was a sin, he replied, "Yes, it is." Lott went on to call for compassion, saying, "You still love that person, and you should not try to mistreat them or treat them as outcasts. You should try to show them a way to deal with that." On the heels of this (grammatically incorrect) moral judgment, Lott went on to analogize homosexuality to alcoholism and, ultimately, to sex addiction and kleptomania.[1]

Setting aside for the moment the internally contradictory nature of these analogies—is homosexuality a sin that calls for forgiveness or a medical condition that calls for treatment and cure?—we marvel at how quickly Lott can move from making a statement of compassion and tolerance to asserting that homosexuals are diseased and, from there, to insinuating that homosexuality is the type of disease that (like kleptomania) inevitably leads to criminal activities. In fairness to Lott, it must be pointed out that his implicit comparison of homosexuals to common criminals is not without some basis in law; in sixteen U.S. states sodomy statutes still criminalize "homosexual behavior." But why in a country that prides itself on the disestablishment of religion should anyone's notion of what counts as sin—and sin is a specifically theological category—be the basis of criminal law?

We also need to ask what it means for the senate majority leader so publicly to espouse these (apparently conflicting) views about homosexuality. Although Lott claimed that his comments were issued in his capacity as a private citizen and believing Christian, his status as an elected official and the national stage from which he was speaking lent his words a moral and political weight not usually accorded the private views of a single citizen. Consequently, we cannot write off Lott's pronouncements as merely private utterances; nor can we dismiss them as just so much political grandstanding, an attempt to curry favor with Christian conservatives, who constitute an important voting block for the Republican party. It may have been both these things, but that does not tell the whole story. Instead, we wonder what Lott's statements about homosexuality tell us about the way tolerance can work to justify hatred, not undercut it. The tough love espoused by Senator Lott may be even tougher than it at first appears. In this book, we explore the limits of religious tolerance in the United States, to show how tolerance can never be an effective replacement for the value of freedom.[2]

A striking example of just how firmly even progressives remain stuck in this limited paradigm of tolerance is the increasing focus on "benign immutable difference" ("can't change, can't help it") as the principal groundwork for fighting discrimination. We analyze the political and moral risks of such a strategy and go on to suggest that a focus on freedom, especially including religious freedom, provides a better means of creating justice than the appeals for tolerance.

The effects of the kind of tolerance offered by the maxim "love the sinner, hate the sin" are far-reaching. They are not confined only to those committed to a Christian theology. Rather, the claims of tolerance underlined by this maxim extend beyond Christianity and self-identified Christians per se to affect multiple facets of American experience—and all this despite the constitutional principle of church-state separation. While the senate majority leader become lay theologian may present a particularly spectacular example, the views Lott expressed are not really all that exceptional.

One of the issues we raise in this book is how it has come to pass that Christian theological pronouncements have become so institutionalized in the official life of the nation that they can be taken for just good old American values. How is it that religion provides the backbone for much of state policy and law around sex? As we show, even the Supreme Court, the institution charged with maintaining the constitutional principle of church-state separation, seems to draw on theology as easily and as often as case law and precedent when rendering decisions that touch on sexual life and homosexual life in particular. This is why, even if you are not Christian and even if you are not particularly religious, you cannot escape the implications of particular interpretations of Christian morality. We need to recognize and confront the following paradox: In a country that proclaims religious freedom, citizens are judged (sometimes even by the highest court in the land) by the standards of a particular religious tradition. Why?

Supreme Court Justice Byron White says this is because "the law is constantly based on notions of morality." And when it comes to morality in American public culture, in the end we're almost always talking about religion. For example, in the aftermath of the 1999 Columbine High School shootings in Littleton, Colorado, the father of one of the victims argued strenuously in a May 1 CNN interview that this kind of tragedy could be prevented only through the teaching of absolute values, and those absolute values must be based on religion and, specifically, on Christianity. While this father was speaking out of the depths of his grief, his yoked assumptions—that American public life requires absolute values and these values are based on religion—are commonplace, whether the location is the mass media, the halls of Congress, or the schoolroom. In fact, a little more than a year later, in July 2000, the Colorado State Board of Education encouraged all Colorado schools to display the words "In God We Trust" in a prominent place. The sponsor of the resolution, who was also chair of the board, wanted these words posted because they were signposts of the moral life. "Our nation has lost its way on the road to virtue and moral character," he said.

As we argue, these quintessential American assumptions about religion, values, and public life are crucially connected to sexuality and its regulation. The secular state's interest in regulating sexuality is an interest in maintaining religious—specifically Christian—authority. In cases concerning homosexuality, the Court refers directly to Christian religious tradition to support its position. The direct appeal to religion is all the more remarkable because the government does not fall back on religion as its primary rationale except when it comes to sex. That is, the state does not commonly call upon religion to justify or provide the final grounds for its decisions in other areas of law or policy. On those other occasions where moral views, explicitly religious or not, are admitted into the decision-making process, they may provide legitimating language in deliberations, but are rarely the driving concern or rationale.

For example, in broader areas of public policy, Christian views on economics are seldom taken into account. The current Bush Administration seems to take Catholic views on abortion and family planning very seriously, but it is interesting to consider how different U.S. economic policy would be if the American Catholic bishops' statements on economics were an integral part of the policy-making process. How much press attention was given to the U.S. Conference of Catholic Bishops' statement in 1999 on debt forgiveness or their appeal to end the death penalty?[3] We would certainly hope that religious views would be taken seriously in public debate about such issues. And we would also hope that a wider range of religious perspectives concerning sexuality would gain a public hearing. Currently, it seems that religious views are taken into public account only around sex and then only if they are conservative views.

Why does religion seem like the natural and appropriate basis for public policies concerning sex, but not for other ethically charged questions? Poverty, the death penalty, the exploitation of the earth's resources, international trade policy—it is not as if these issues have no moral bearing. And yet religion is not the primary language for debating them. Why do the assumptions change when it comes to sex?

It is crucial to illuminate the relations among religion, morality, and sex as they come together in the context of U.S. public life, especially because time after time and issue after issue, it seems that sexual matters become the measures of an individual's—and even a nation's—overall morality. Moreover, sexuality figures, sometimes obliquely and sometimes explicitly, in a series of issues that at first glance would appear to have nothing whatsoever to do with sex.

There are many examples to choose from here, but welfare policy is an especially important case, because so few people would expect such a major economic and social policy to turn on sex. However, much of the congressional debate about the Personal Responsibility and Work Opportunity Reconciliation Act of 1996 (also known as "welfare reform") focused on questions of sexual irresponsibility and teenage motherhood. President Clinton's advocacy for the bill was largely framed around the need for sexual responsibility, as when he said that no social problem "stands in our way of achieving our goals for America more than the epidemic of teen pregnancy."[4] This obsessive focus on sex was even extended in a little-known portion of the law that offered states millions of dollars in federal matching grants for sex education in public schools, but only on the condition that they make abstinence the exclusive aim of their sex education efforts. According to the 1996 federal guidelines, children are to be taught that "sexual activity outside the context of marriage is likely to have harmful psychological and physical effects." When the law came up for renewal in 2002, in addition to continuing funding for abstinence education, the Bush Administration also proposed a new funding initiative for marriage education in public schools. Why were either of these provisions part of a bill about changing the way that we as a society address poverty? What's sex got to do with it?

In the United States sex is the site of often contradictory moral worries. On the one hand, sex is sometimes dismissed (and also justified) as merely a private affair. On the other hand, sex is also invested with amazing and paradoxical powers. For example, sexual relations are thought to be foundational to family and, by extension, to the American nation. At the same time sex is thought to be so powerful that it threatens to dissolve family ties and thereby unravel the nation itself.

Our own view is somewhat more skeptical. We suspect that sex is not an all-powerful solvent that can—as people often say—"destroy Western civilization as we know it." However, once one accepts the terms of this fantasy, it becomes imperative to control sex, regulating where it can happen and between whom. Its power must be contained and "domesticated." This way of thinking about sex and its potentially destructive power serves to justify extensive regulations on sex and sexuality in the United States—regulations that otherwise seem at odds with the high value supposedly set on freedom in the United States. Sex is one area where this ideal of freedom does not seem to prevail. (Indeed, contemporary descriptions of the sexual revolution of the 1960s and 1970s would have us believe that, if anything, there is too much sexual freedom in the United States.)

Sexual regulations are not just about sex. By regulating sex, the state attempts to regulate family life and American social relations more broadly. Through myriad regulations the state actually defines what counts as family. Regulation becomes a form of recognition for those who fit into the category of "family." But why should the state get to decide who is a family? Here is where the rhetoric of family values once again meets the rhetoric of sexual regulation. Family solves the sex problem. It is supposed to domesticate sexuality without its participants having entirely to give up on the American discourse of freedom. In its idealized form, the family is free from government interference, because family matters, including sexual relations, are supposed to be protected by privacy.

Privacy establishes a zone within which certain activities that would not be permitted "in public" are legitimated. Most Americans think that privacy is actually a fairly capacious category. But in reality, many ostensibly private places—such as homes—are scarcely afforded the protections of privacy. For example, American common sense says that sexual relations between consenting adults are their own business, and as long as they conduct these relations in private, they are free to act as they please. Many consensual sexual acts, however, whether "homosexual" or "heterosexual," undertaken by Americans in their own homes are actually illegal. Sodomy laws, for instance, cover a wide range of sexual activities between same-sex as well as cross-sex partners. If the sexual acts between President Clinton and Monica Lewinsky had taken place in a state with sodomy laws like Virginia, rather than in the District of Columbia (which has no such laws), both Clinton and Lewinsky could have been charged with sodomy. This expansive reach is not just the purview of sodomy statutes, which criminalize certain sexual acts (even if they take place in the home), but also of laws against adultery, which remain on the books in several states (albeit largely unenforced). In both these instances (laws against sodomy and laws against adultery) a private dwelling may or may not offer a firewall against state interference in the sexual lives of its inhabitants.

Whatever constitutional right to privacy has been read into the U.S. Constitution is ultimately based on presumptions about married couples. When the Supreme Court struck down Connecticut's ban on birth control in *Griswold v. Connecticut* (1965), it did so because the ban violated the privacy rights of the marital couple.[5] This recognition of privacy as a fundamental right did not extend to the sexual lives of unmarried persons. It wasn't until 1972 in *Eisenstadt v. Baird* that the Court declared unconstitutional a Massachusetts statute prohibiting distribution of contraceptive devices to unmarried persons. A woman's right to abortion as articulated in the *Roe v. Wade* (1973) decision was an extension of *Griswold* and assumed that a woman could exercise her conscience, but she was expected to do so in consultation with her physician.[6] No wonder the Supreme Court has upheld many states' restrictions on exercising this right, such as requiring women to consult with a doctor twice before the procedure, or mandating that young women obtain their parents' permission.

Not even the freedom of the marital couple is a freedom without limits; rather, it is carefully circumscribed and, ultimately, conditional. "Conditional" in this sense: the benefits that playing by the rules of family afford—such as a limited freedom and the feeling of privacy—are not once and for all, but may be taken away as conditions change. Should a family fall on hard times and require governmental economic support or public housing, for example, it becomes liable to invasive forms of state supervision. In fact, virtually any change that a family goes through—whether it be something as happy as the adoption of children or as emotionally wrenching as divorce—is subject to state scrutiny and control. As we will discuss in greater detail, when the Supreme Court upheld a state's right to ban homosexual sodomy in 1986, it reasoned that privacy rights do not extend to homosexual sodomy precisely because "none of the fundamental rights announced in this Court's prior cases involving family relationships, marriage, or procreation bear any resemblance to the right [to 'consensual homosexual sodomy'] asserted in this case."[7]

One of our fundamental concerns, then, is that promises of "freedom" and "privacy"—promises supposedly made to every American by virtue of being a citizen—are actually held out as rewards, not rights, and only to those who belong to the right kind of family. What kind of freedom is this when enjoyment of it requires subjection to narrow, exclusionary, and even sectarian understandings of who and what constitute family? This social contract really contracts, limiting the possibilities for freedom for all Americans.

We are particularly interested in the way that these dynamics play out in the case of homosexuality and what is commonly called "gay rights," but we want to point out that our concerns are not just about homosexuals or homosexuality. We're interested in thinking about the conditions of sexual freedom for everyone, not just for gay men and lesbians. We focus on homosexuality because it is an overburdened site of moral concern and hence can be a particularly illuminating case study of sexual regulation.

Attacking homosexuality functions to draw attention away from other no less fundamental challenges to older sexual orthodoxies and arrangements: the changing role of women; increasing numbers of single-parent households; the lowering of social stigmas around out-of-wedlock childbirth. Many of these changes, although cast in moral terms by conservatives who wish simply to return to the way we (never) were, are the result of major economic and social changes.[8] Despite the fact that the large majority of Americans have pragmatically adjusted to and even embraced these transformations, there remains for many people some sense of disquiet about how they are living their own lives.[9]

When it comes to heterosexuality, there are still many Americans who believe that sex outside very circumscribed parameters, such as marriage, is, if not morally wrong, at least morally questionable. Yet, in actual experience, these same Americans often have sex outside marriage, for example, and the world doesn't end. That people can believe both these things—sex is morally dangerous and utterly ordinary—and have trouble letting go of either could not be better illustrated than by those members of Congress, such as the former Speaker of the House, Newt Gingrich, who are deeply dedicated to a conservative sexual morality (at least in terms of seeking to enforce it as social policy) but are also deeply committed (at least in terms of doing it repeatedly) to sex outside the bounds of that morality. We might just label Gingrich a hypocrite, but the dilemma we are sketching goes beyond hypocrisy. How many young people (and not-so-young people) are there in America who have sex in its various forms and yet cannot shake the vague sense that they are doing something wrong?

Without a doubt, the past three decades have witnessed important shifts in public attitudes toward sex and sexuality, but how far do these shifts go? If Americans in general are much more relaxed about some aspects of heterosexuality—sex outside marriage, cohabitation, contraception—many remain troubled about some kinds of sex, and homosexuality becomes a particular trouble spot on which to focus their worries. This moral disquiet gets represented in the division between hetero and homo, which substitutes for the opposition "good versus bad." Regulating homosexuality helps to affirm for ourselves and for others that we have not abandoned all our moral principles. We still hold some lines, such that, even if most of us violate traditional sexual morality on a regular basis, we haven't lost our way entirely. Moreover, we can assure ourselves that so long as Americans live by an appropriate sexual code, we need not worry about American moral health in other areas like economic policy.

We not only believe that worrying about sex becomes a way not to worry (or even think about) other pressing issues; we also believe that many common American concerns about sex are misplaced. We take sex and questions of sexual justice seriously, but we're concerned that the way in which sex is usually argued about in public debates actually distracts from such fundamental questions. We advocate an alternative set of moral possibilities for valuing sex and valuing sex differently, even as we recognize that in many public debates about sex, some moral perspectives (the ones we are advancing, for instance) are ruled out in advance as no morality at all.

As we have suggested, the current commonsense view is that morality is based on religion and is primarily about regulation—self-regulation in the form of conscience and the direct and indirect regulation of others. For example, when confronted by a morally contentious issue, many Americans think it is appropriate to look for a consensus among various religious traditions. Locating moral propositions on which different religions seem to agree offers a way to assert the moral coherence of a particular view; it invests a particular argument with an air of objectivity and fairness.[10] But why assume that morality in the public sphere is about moral agreement rather than moral debate? We do not object to having moral questions inform public debate, but we do object when morality is thought to mean religion, and only religion, and morality is thought to be singular rather than plural and open to debate.

Different religious traditions offer different ways of thinking about the good life, but one need not be a person of religious faith in order to be ethically engaged. Religion is one way of thinking about morality, but is not the measure of it. This might sound like an argument for stricter enforcement of church-state separation, but recognizing ethics that are distinct from religious views does not necessarily mean mandating public secularism, at least not in the ways the religion-secularism distinction is currently understood.[11]

Religion and secularism are generally taken to be in opposition to each other, which results in common misperceptions across the political spectrum. First, from the point of view of those who are religious, making room for nonreligious ethical debate seems to entail diminishing the space for religious expression. But recognizing secular morality as morality and giving it public weight do not necessarily demean religion or religious people; such public recognition adds another set of voices to an ongoing conversation.

Second, many social progressives are leery of making any kind of ethical claim for fear of playing into the hands of religious conservatives. Because the American Right, particularly the Christian Right, so easily and often draws upon the language of religion to justify its moral claims, it often seems that resisting the Right necessarily requires resisting religion. As a result, when public discourse is structured so that it feels impossible to make a values claim that is not religious in some general sense, the only alternative appears to be enforcing strict secularism and rejecting religion. But this leaves little or no room for progressives—religious or otherwise—to make clear what they value and why.

The problem is not religion per se. After all, although this fact is often forgotten (by both the Right and the Left) progressive politics in the United States has not always been uniformly "against" religion.[12] Just think of the rich history of progressive movements for African American civil rights that were grounded in the Black Church, the movements for economic justice grounded in the Catholic worker movement in the United States and Catholic base communities in Central America, the long-standing tradition of Jewish progressive politics, and the Quaker movements on behalf of abolition and against war. These social justice movements, their histories and achievements, should make clear that the entry of religion into politics and public life is not in and of itself conservative.

Building on this insight, we are taking a different tack than those who argue simply for a stricter enforcement of the separation of church and state. We desire more public space for secularism, space that would recognize secularism as a legitimate moral stance. But we simultaneously desire more religious freedom (which is not the same thing as advocating more religion). These two desires are neither mutually exclusive nor necessarily antagonistic. We want the freedom not to be religious and the freedom to be religious differently. And we want both these positions to count as the possible basis for moral claims and public policy. If the United States is to realize its claims regarding the free exercise of religion, then no single set of religious moral prescriptions (or proscriptions) can be the basis of public policy or national identity.

We think it's important for Americans to come to terms with the fact that Christianity, and often conservative Christianity, functions as the yardstick and measure of what counts as "religion" and "morality" in America. To be traditionally American is to be Christian in a certain way. Part of our critique of American secularism, then, is that it is not really secular. When the president takes his oath of office and makes his inaugural address, there are always references to God, and we all know which God is being invoked (after all, every president of the United States has been Christian in some way, and only one has been Catholic). And when the Christian Coalition talks about "taking back America," they want to enforce this connection between Americanness and particular Christian commitments.

What does this mean for non-Christians or even for those who are Christian in another way? Under these circumstances, those who are different will always and only be "minorities" to be "tolerated" within the "general" American public. Dissenting ethical perspectives can be admitted to the public square only on the condition that they overlap in some way with this dominant framework. If there is insufficient overlap, these ethical counterclaims will be placed outside the realm of recognizable values. They simply are not values.

So, for example, African American Christian ethicist Katie Cannon argues that Black Womanist ethics, even when they are explicitly theological, are often not recognized as moral. Instead, they are labeled immoral or amoral precisely because they may criticize some of the basic assumptions of American life, such as the American economic system and its idealization of the freely acting individual with a multitude of choices. This idealization can hardly be meaningful for a community-based ethical tradition, like the one on which Cannon draws, that is grounded in the moral accomplishment of those persons who have often been denied the right to individual freedom or free choice in U.S. society.[13]

In short, for dissenting views to be heard currently, they have to speak the language of a consensus from which they are already excluded. The price of refusing to speak this common language is either not to be recognized at all or to be recognized only so as to be dismissed as an "extremist." And for this we're supposed to be grateful. Such are the limits of tolerance in America. What does it feel like to be on the receiving end of this tolerance? Does it really feel any different from contempt or exclusion? Can one actually love the sinner while hating the sin?

In the five chapters to follow, we lay out our case for the vital links between sexual freedom and religious freedom one step at a time. Each chapter builds on the analyses and arguments of the one that precedes it. The deliberate sequencing and pacing of our five chapters are warranted by the nature of our arguments; we recognize that the claims at the center of this book are counterintuitive, running up against deeply ingrained practices and habits of thought concerning sex, religion, and what it means to be an American. We will show how many of the democratic rights and privileges taken for granted by most Americans are actually narrowed and parceled out in exclusionary and unjust ways.

We are not concerned only with official—that is, governmental—regulation of homosexuality. Rather, the case study approach that guides this book leads us to consider how homosexuality and gay rights are discussed, debated, and regulated in a wide range of public arenas: from the Supreme Court to the halls of Congress to state legislatures; from mass circulation magazines to television talk shows.

In both chapters 1 and 2, we will spend some time unpacking—and criticizing—the popular assumptions undergirding discussions of homosexuality. We are interested in showing how and why religion provides the context for talking about, fighting over, and regulating sex in the United States. Together, these first two chapters will outline the limits on freedom in the contemporary United States.

Chapter 1, "Getting Religion," focuses on one of the founding ideals of American democracy: church-state separation. This is an ideal underrealized in practice.

Particularly when it comes to debates over sex, the line separating church and state blurs dangerously. This is precisely what happened in the two Supreme Court cases discussed in chapter 1, *Bowers v. Hardwick* (1986) and *Romer v. Evans* (1996). Both cases concern homosexuality; and in both, we suggest that specifically Christian ideas about sexual morality and the value of tolerance came to play a surprising role in the Court's reasoning.

We continue our analysis of tolerance and its limitations in chapter 2, "What's Wrong with Tolerance?" Here our case studies are drawn not from court cases, but from the court of public opinion. We examine media coverage of some highly publicized killings, such as the 1998 murder of gay college student Matthew Shepard. We do so in order to trace how public understanding of hate and what have been labeled "hate crimes" is filtered through and, we will argue, actually impeded by a vocabulary of "tolerance." Our argument in this chapter thus constitutes a sharp departure from the American commonsense view that tolerance is the solution, or antidote, to bigotry and hatred.

Our overarching goal in this chapter is not simply to indicate how a logic of tolerance shapes—and restricts—public conversations and even policies about homosexuality. We also, and perhaps more significantly, want to demonstrate how public debates about any number of morally contentious issues—homosexuality and gay rights among them—become part of a process of constituting "the public." The stakes here are high—and are not just about homosexuality. Attention to how homosexuality is talked about and represented in any number of public venues allows us to glimpse larger processes of American national identity formation and thereby to ask some difficult questions: How are the contours of American belonging shaped and reshaped? What public language is available for talking about what we value and why? And just who are the "we" who talk and talk some more?

The question of how "the public" is constituted is interrogated from a slightly different vantage point in chapter 3, "Not Born That Way." Here we sketch the most common ways advocates of gay and lesbian rights have sought to make their case in the public square. By and large, mainstream gay rights rhetoric has attempted to short-circuit moral debates over homosexuality with an appeal to "nature." That is, advocates of gay and lesbian rights have tended to assert that homosexuals are "born that way." They commonly underline this assertion with an analogy between sexuality and race, going on from there to call for tolerance for the "unchosen" difference of homosexuality. We believe that such analogies—between sexual identity and racial identity and, from there, between discrimination against homosexuals and discrimination against people of color—are not just deficient, they are dangerous. They do not promote sexual freedom, and they can do damage to racial justice.

We want to recast the debate, shifting from arguments over origins (is homosexuality "in born" or "chosen"?) and analogies to race to robust public discussions of sexual ethics. In our view, it does not matter how one becomes homosexual, *because there is nothing wrong with homosexuality*. In one sense, our argument in chapter 3 is just that simple. Thus, we wonder what new possibilities for thinking about, and achieving, sexual freedom might be gained by connecting sexual freedom to religious freedom. Such a conceptual shift, we argue, would also be of value in public debates over race and racial justice. We believe that the freedom to be different and act differently should not depend on whether or not an individual is "born that way."

Our proposal to make religion the ground of sexual freedom, rather than the *justification* for sexual regulation, is not just an attempt to intervene in contemporary debates over homosexuality and gay rights. It also represents an attempt to rethink some important American values: religion and freedom. Accordingly, in chapter 4, "The Free Exercise of Sex," we detail how and why religious freedom and sexual freedom in America are conjoined projects—or should be so linked. As will become clear, the freedom we are imagining and advocating here is not the freedom promised by liberal tolerance, which makes room for homosexuals on the condition that they become "just like everyone else." This model of freedom might eventually grant full social recognition to those homosexuals who want what everyone else is supposed to want (from marriage and family to the right to serve openly in the U.S. military). But what room is left for those homosexuals *and* heterosexuals who value different things?

Too often, as the "born that way" argument for gay rights reveals, gay and lesbian advocates and allies have been willing to cede questions of sexual values to those who think homosexuality is "wrong" and sex is for marriage—or it is for nothing at all. In our fifth chapter, "Valuing Sex," we do not retreat from the question of what we value and why. Instead, we make a case for sex, including homosexual sex. Sex, we argue, can be a site for the production of values. To support this claim, we turn to the rich varieties of gay and lesbian community formation and consider how sex, precisely because it is embedded in interpersonal relations, can help constitute new forms of social life and belonging.

Ultimately, this is a book about democratic possibility. Over the course of our five linked chapters, we move from critique to constructive engagement. We do not seek simply to expose and criticize the limitations on sexual and religious freedom in contemporary America, but to offer proposals for a different kind of future. One of the reasons to protect and promote freedom is that freedom allows for the development of moral alternatives. Correspondingly, if we are to expand the possibilities for freedom in America, we must also expand the ways in which we talk about and enact values, including sexual values.

1 Getting Religion

One of the most puzzling, yet persistent, features of public life in the United States is how quickly talking about sex turns into talking about religion and, conversely, how quickly talking about religion turns into talking about sex. It is not simply that religion is the context for public debates and policy making around sex; rather, in a fundamental sense, the secular state's regulation of the sexual life of its citizens is actually religion by other means. Even the constitutional principle of church-state separation seems to give way when it comes to sex. In this chapter, we look at cases in which the Supreme Court, which is charged with maintaining this important constitutional bedrock, uses religion as a basis for rendering decisions about sex. But why? What makes sex so troublesome, so dangerous, that religion seems to be the only answer?

The claim that sex is inherently "trouble" is a baseline of American public discourse about sex. According to this view, sex by its very nature is so morally fraught as always to require a chaperone. We certainly do not dispute the immense symbolic weight that sexual practices and identities carry in the contemporary moment. We want to ask, however, why this is the case. Why sex? Why religion?

It is true that sexual practices and preferences attract a kind of critical scrutiny (from oneself and from others) that other bodily practices and appetites do not. However, as a number of historians have shown, while sexuality has often been regulated, the form and content of these regulations have varied. The same kinds of moral meanings have not been assigned to sexual acts from culture to culture. Additionally, even within a given culture, sexual acts take on different meanings over time. Thus, it is a mistake to assume that the moral meaning assigned to particular acts and desires today has remained constant for all time.[1]

Contemporary conversations about sex and sexual values in the United States are often impeded by these linked assumptions: sex is a problem, and a moral problem at that; it has always been a problem; religion is the solution. We disagree. These assumptions ultimately misrecognize both sex and ethics, seeing one as always and everywhere a problem for the other. Sex is no more a "problem" that requires solving than religion is the necessary solution.

Anthropologist Gayle Rubin helpfully identifies some persistent conceptual stumbling blocks that get in the way of thinking about sex.[2] These impediments include both sexual essentialism and what she calls "sex negativity." An essentialist view of sex sees it as some naturally occurring, presocial force internal to an individual but outside history. Further, this sexuality-as-essence constitutes a powerful life force, bubbling forth to shape individuals and affect the societies they inhabit. Within this worldview, sexuality is not just powerful; it is dangerous. It is held to be dangerous, in part, because it is conceptualized as a biological force existing outside or "before" society and the rules that govern it. Left unchecked, sex threatens the moral order of things. This is sex negativity, the belief, as Rubin quips, that sex is "guilty until proven innocent" (11).

Against this backdrop of sexual essentialism and sex negativity, the vast array of moral rules and regulations governing sexual conduct represents attempts to keep sex in line and society on course. In the United States, these moral rules are often enforced by the state. Religion continues to supply the rationale for the state regulation of sexuality. At first glance, this might seem like a startling claim. After all, the United States is supposed to be a secular society, organized on the principle of church-state separation. And yet, religion—specifically Christianity—shapes legislation, public policy, and even jurisprudence around sex. One of the reasons religion can continue to operate this way, even in the face of the official doctrine of church-state separation, is that the assumptions that underlie sexual regulation are so deeply embedded that people no longer recognize them as being derived from religious thought.

The usual story told about secularization in Western societies is that over the course of the seventeenth and eighteenth centuries, as the modern period developed, there was a progressive retreat of religion from public life, including, most prominently, from the workings of the market and government. Tasks that were once delegated to Church and Crown came to be assigned, via linked processes of secularization and democratization, to the state. Religion, previously such a force in public life, was pushed to the background, to a newly privatized zone of family, morality, and questions of conscience. So the story goes, but it only goes so far.[3]

We want to tell a different story. Underreported in the usual way of telling this story of modernity are all the ways in which religious ideas about the body have continued to be enforced by the newly secularized state. This, then, is the "afterlife" of religion in modernity: secularization has not so much meant the *retreat* of religion from the public sphere as its *reinvention*. This reinvention is accomplished through a conflation of religion and morality, in which morality is assumed to be the essence of religion and, conversely, moral proclamation can be a means of invoking religion without directly naming it. In other words, under cover of an official secularism, particular religious claims about "the good life," the way things are or should be, can still remain operative.

These processes do not work the same way in all Western societies. In the particular case of the United States, the dominant framework for morality is not simply "religious" or even "Christian," but is specifically Protestant. Protestant dominance does not mean that other religious traditions within Christianity and sometimes within Judaism are not given any space in American public life; rather, the *unstated* religious assumptions of U.S. secularism are specifically Protestant. The conflation of religion and morality that produces these unstated assumptions is part of a process of historical amnesia. In the United States, religion—Protestantism, that is—works to supply the moral foundation all the more thoroughly because its specific religious lineage is often forgotten.

Sodomy laws are a fascinating example of this forgetfulness in action. On the one hand, in enforcing sodomy laws, the secular state is enforcing specifically religious ideas about "natural" and "unnatural" sexual acts and appetites. On the other hand, the secular state understands itself to be doing so not in the name of religion per se, but in the cause of a universal morality. And yet, time and again particular religious interpretations provide the state's last best defense for its policies concerning sex.

As a way to expose how particular Christian claims are at work in the American state's ongoing regulation of sexuality, we take a close look at two Supreme Court cases, both of which concern homosexuality: *Bowers v. Hardwick* (1986) and *Romer v. Evans* (1996). The outcome of both cases is by now well known. In *Bowers v. Hardwick,* the Supreme Court upheld the constitutionality of sodomy statutes, finding that states did have the right and even the moral interest to regulate and criminalize consensual sexual activity between persons of the same sex. The majority opinion in *Romer v. Evans,* by contrast, overturned Colorado's antigay Amendment 2. The Court ruled 6 to 3 that Amendment 2, which won the support of a majority of Colorado voters in a 1992 statewide referendum, unconstitutionally denied equal protection to homosexuals.

At first glance, it seems as if these two cases resulted in completely different judgments—the one, a defeat for gay rights, the other, an unalloyed victory. But on a closer view, some surprising convergences may be found. We do not pretend that our analyses of these two cases are exhaustive. Nor are we seeking to offer a close constitutional analysis; we are neither legal scholars nor constitutional historians. Instead we are offering a rhetorical analysis in order to lay bare a cluster of assumptions at work in both *Hardwick* and *Romer*. Examining the logic behind the Supreme Court's decisions in these two cases helps to illuminate the links outlined above among religion, sexual regulation, and the secular state. As we shall see, when it comes to homosexuality at least, often what the Court dispenses is not justice but religion.

Bowers v. Hardwick

Nowhere is the state's dependence on religion to justify sexual regulation made more clear than in *Bowers v. Hardwick*. This 1986 case concerned the constitutionality of Georgia's sodomy statute. *Hardwick* revolved around the government's right to regulate, in Justice Byron White's words, certain kinds of "private sexual conduct between consenting adults."[4] Apparently some sex acts are so far from being moral that even privacy and consent do not insulate them from government interference. Georgia's statute was not the only one in dispute, however; the Supreme Court's decision would also determine the constitutionality of a patchwork of sodomy laws in force elsewhere in the United States. At the time *Hardwick* reached the highest court, twenty-five states had sodomy laws in some form. Today, more than fifteen years after the *Hardwick* decision, sodomy statutes remain on the books and in force in sixteen states and in the U.S. military.

In the first]volume of his three-volume *History of Sexuality*, Michel Foucault famously describes sodomy as "that utterly confused category."[5] Something of this confusion may be seen in the various state laws against consensual sodomy. Just which sexual acts are prohibited varies from state to state. In some states, sodomy is defined exclusively as anal sex between men; in other states, sodomy refers to any act of anal sex or oral sex, no matter the sex (male or female) of the partici- pants. Notably, in every state that still has a sodomy statute, the law criminalizes consensual sex between men; by comparison, the legal status of consensual sex be- tween women and consensual oral or anal sex between men and women differs from state to state.

The case that became *Bowers v. Hardwick* began when a Georgia man, Michael Hardwick, was arrested in the fall of 1982 for an act of oral sex performed in the privacy of his own bedroom. The police literally entered his bedroom to deliver a warrant for Hardwick's arrest in conjunction with an earlier event. As legal scholar Kendall Thomas explains, "Hardwick's arrest in the privacy of his bedroom was the culmination of a . . . series of events which were set in motion" when Hardwick was ticketed for drinking in public by an Atlanta police officer named K. R. Torick.[6] It was this same officer who would later arrest Hardwick and a male companion at Hardwick's home.

While the ultimate legal question in *Hardwick* was whether the constitutional right to privacy protected homosexuals in their sexual acts, the "prehistory" of Hardwick's arrest for sodomy had a decidedly public backdrop—outside a gay bar in Atlanta where Hardwick worked. Torick "stopped Hardwick after seeing him throw a beer bottle into a trashcan outside the bar." According to Hardwick's ac- count of the incident, Torick then "'made me get in the car and asked what I was doing. I told him that I worked there, which immediately identified me as a ho- mosexual, because he knew it was a homosexual bar.' Torick then issued Hardwick a ticket for drinking in public" (Thomas 1438).[7] After a series of bureaucratic errors, the ticket for public drinking led to an arrest warrant for failure to appear in court (Hardwick had been given the wrong date for his court appearance), and this war- rant was the ostensible reason Officer Torick ended up at Hardwick's bedroom door approximately one month after their first fateful meeting.

Certainly, the circumstances of Hardwick's arrest indicate how little meaning the right to privacy has for gay people. But more than that, the initial summons, issued for "drinking in public," also reveals the limits on gay people's *public* mobility. The freedom of movement—to go in and out of bars and restaurants without fear of harassment, to move in and around one's place of work without worry— is something many Americans take for granted. This is not a freedom always available to gay people.

After the police entered his bedroom, Hardwick and his male companion were arrested and charged under Georgia's sodomy statute. Although the Fulton County District Attorney ultimately declined to prosecute, Hardwick decided to challenge the statute on constitutional grounds for its criminalization of consensual sodomy. The case made its way through state and federal courts to the U.S. Supreme Court.

By a 5 to 4 majority, the Court upheld Georgia's sodomy statute and, with it, the sexual regulation of bodies—of some bodies, that is. For, even as the Court affirmed the state's right to regulate its citizens' bodies, this was no blank check. The Court affirmed the constitutionality of sodomy statutes, at least insofar as they applied to "consensual homosexual sodomy":

The Constitution does not confer a fundamental right upon homosexuals to engage in sodomy. None of the fundamental rights announced in this Court's prior cases involving family relationships, marriage, or procreation bear any resemblance to the right asserted in this case. And any claim that those cases stand for the proposition that any kind of private sexual conduct between consenting adults is constitutionally insulated from state proscription is unsupportable.[8]

While the Court addresses the question of homosexual sodomy in such strong language, the legal fate of some other bodies in their sexual acts is dispatched to a footnote. Writing for the majority, Justice White simply states: "We express no opinion on the constitutionality of the Georgia statute as applied to other acts of sodomy" (*Hardwick* 188n2).

We are left to fill in the blank for those "other acts of sodomy" Justice White will not or cannot utter in the open: heterosexual. Lord Alfred Douglas once famously described homosexuality as "the love that dare not speak its name." By contrast, heterosexuality seems to be the identity that *need* not speak its name; it just goes without saying. (In fact, there may be no surer way to call your heterosexuality into question than to proclaim it too openly.[9]) Heterosexuality can go without saying in all the mundane practices of everyday life: it is taken for granted in all kinds of casual conversations, whether struck up between strangers or between acquaintances, about weekend plans, romantic status, or favorite movie stars. Similarly, the Court manages to talk about heterosexual sodomy without having to name it directly.

This silence on the matter of heterosexual sodomy—"no opinion"—was not an innocent one. Rather, it ignored the Georgia statute as written. A 1968 amendment to Georgia's sodomy statute made the state's prohibition on sodomy neutral on the question of homo- or heterosexuality: "A person commits the offense of sodomy when he performs or submits to any act involving the sex organs of one person and the mouth or anus of the other" (qtd. in majority opinion, *Hardwick* 188n1[a]). In other words, according to the state of Georgia, sodomy was an equal opportunity offense. Anyone could commit it; the legal prohibition on it did not discriminate, at least in theory, between kinds of sexual persons. What the statute did do was discriminate between good and bad sexual conduct, turning this moral hierarchy into a legal distinction between licit and illicit acts.

Moreover, privacy was not in and of itself a shield from the state and its moral claims on the citizen-body. Georgia's sodomy statute asserted the state's right to regulate bodies in their sexual acts no matter the participants' sex (male or female), no matter their sexual self-identifications (homosexual or heterosexual), and no matter their place of activity (private or public). Certainly, the broad reach of Georgia's sodomy statute was pointedly underlined by the place of Hardwick's arrest—his own bedroom.

The vicissitudes of privacy rights were further illuminated when a heterosexual couple—identified in the Court papers as "John and Mary Doe"—signed onto the case as coplaintiffs, claiming that the double edge of the criminal statute and Hardwick's arrest under it had effectively regulated their own private sexual conduct in advance. However, a lower court held that because the couple "had neither sustained, nor were in immediate danger of sustaining, any direct injury from enforcement of the statute" (*Hardwick* 188n2), they had no standing in the case. It seems that there was no expectation on the part of the lower court that the statute would be enforced against a heterosexual couple. The Supreme Court upheld the District Court's decision in this matter, reinforcing the Does' separation from the case by remanding John and Mary Doe to that same second footnote. Keeping heterosexuality out of any immediate danger became, quite literally, the case's subtext.

How is it possible that the highest court in the land, whose responsibility it is to interpret and apply the law, could simply ignore the Georgia statute in question—even as the Justices quoted from it? There is no ambiguity in the statute as it was amended in 1968; it applied to anyone who committed what the state of Georgia broadly defined as "sodomy." This squeamishness about applying the statute to heterosexuals was reenacted in 1998, when the Georgia Supreme Court finally ruled, in *Powell v. State of Georgia*, that the sodomy statute was unconstitutional. All too predictably, this grew out of the state's failed prosecution of Anthony Juan Powell for the rape and aggravated (forcible) sodomy of his seventeen-year-old niece. He was also charged with and convicted of consensual sodomy, but the Georgia Supreme Court ruled that in this case, unlike *Hardwick*, "such behavior between adults in private is recognized as a private matter."

The Supreme Court's refusal to apply this law neutrally in 1986—to both homosexuals like Michael Hardwick and heterosexuals like John and Mary Doe—is a perfect example of what social theorists Lauren Berlant and Michael Warner have called "heteronormativity."[10] Heteronormativity is not synonymous with heterosexuality. There are forms of heterosexual practice ("polygamy," for example) that are not heteronormative. Heteronormativity describes the moral and conceptual centrality of heterosexuality in contemporary American life. The Court's interest in upholding heteronormativity obliged it to overlook or wish away non-normative heterosexuality of the sort practiced by the Does—and by many other self-identified heterosexuals too. (When the protective screen is lifted, as when the Georgia Supreme Court was forced in 1988 to look at a case that involved only heterosexual sodomy, privacy is suddenly found to cover such acts, bringing the screen down yet again.)

But perhaps this states the matter too bluntly. It is not necessarily the case that the U.S. Supreme Court consciously set out to defend the normative status of heterosexuality. As Berlant and Warner argue, part of what makes heteronormativity so powerful is that it depends upon and works through a set of *unconscious* assumptions. That is, heterosexuality forms the "basic idiom" of everyday life (Berlant and Warner 548n2).

In *Hardwick,* the majority's refusal to acknowledge heterosexual sodomy effectively creates a screen behind which a potentially "deviant" heterosexuality goes unnoticed and unmarked. The veil of privacy extended to heterosexuals in this case does not simply protect the marital couple; it also protects the category of heterosexuality as a normative principle and does so by concealing any possible overlap between heterosexuality and homosexuality. Specifically, it denies that an "act involving the sex organs of one person and the mouth or anus of the other" could be the same (at least in legal terms) whether it was committed by homosexual or heterosexual partners.

One effect of the Court's bracketing of *"other* acts of sodomy"(emphasis added)—its separation of heterosexuality from homosexuality—was to narrow the statute's range and, with it, the state's regulatory reach. Another was to intensify a link between particular kinds of conduct and particular kinds of identity. Sodomy statutes reflect an older way of thinking about sex and bodies—one that pivots around permitted and proscribed acts. The Court's parsing of the difference between sodomitical acts the state should and could constitutionally regulate ("homosexual sodomy") and those about which the Court has "no opinion" (the never named "heterosexual sodomy") indicates a more recent concern with status or identity. When Justice White distinguishes bodies and acts that are insulated from state interference from bodies and acts that are not, he links the legal status of a particular sexual act (is it licit or illicit?) to the kinds of persons committing the act. Not every act of sodomy is equally bad, he seems to be claiming; the identity of the participants lends some bodies an alibi of innocence. One of the many odd features of the majority's decision in *Hardwick* is that its legal analysis of sexual acts is overtaken by an underlying preoccupation with questions of sexual identity. This tension—conduct or status, act or identity—returns with a vengeance in *Romer*. But before turning to *Romer*, we must first consider the role of religion in *Hardwick*.

Morality was at the core of the Court's reasoning. But whose morality? The Court, both in the majority opinion written by White and Chief Justice Warren Burger's concurring opinion, appealed to the weight of moral tradition, whose universal obviousness seemed to require little further argument. In a race through Western history, both Justices point to the history of proscriptions against homosexual sodomy and argue on that basis for the continuing moral claims against such conduct. White moves quickly from what he terms the "ancient roots" of such proscriptions to laws of the original thirteen states to there being "no cognizable roots in the language or design of the Constitution" for homosexual sodomy as a fundamental liberty (*Hardwick* 194). In White's view, the history of prohibitions on sodomy is an unbroken one, and against this backdrop, to assert that "a right to engage in such conduct is 'deeply rooted in this Nation's history and tradition' or 'implicit in the concept of ordered liberty' is, at best, facetious" (194).

Although White will not fully name or cite the "notions of morality" that inform and shape the law (and which the dissenting Justices actually call him to do), he nevertheless thinks the moral claims of law a reason sufficient unto itself: "The law, however, is constantly based on notions of morality, and if all laws representing essentially moral choices are to be invalidated under the Due Process Clause, the courts will be very busy indeed" (196). If we look at the "Nation's history and tradition," we must acknowledge that the continuous record White poses is one shaped by and through Christian theological responses to sodomy and, in particular, to conceptions of the ordered body that emerged out of the Reformed Protestant tradition. Of course, unlike White, Christian theology is not exactly unfazed by the specter of "heterosexual" sodomy. There is a long history of Christian worries about "unnatural" sexual practices between men and women.[11] Why, we wonder, is White willing to overlook the "ancient roots" of prohibitions on sodomy between men and women, when he will not grant the same moral flexibility to sex between men?

If Justice White is so fully in thrall to the obvious that he cannot or will not mention by name just whose "notions of morality" and whose "essentially moral choices" the law represents—choices and notions that he, in the name of the law, is sustaining—Justice Burger, in his concurring opinion, cuts to the chase. In Burger's thumbnail history of sodomy and Western civilization, he writes:

As the Court notes . . . the proscriptions against sodomy have very "ancient roots." Decisions of individuals relating to homosexual conduct have been subject to state intervention throughout the history of Western Civilization. Condemnation of those practices is firmly rooted in Judaeo- Christian moral and ethical standards. Homosexual sodomy was a capital crime under Roman law. . . . During the English Reformation when powers of the ecclesiastical courts were transferred to the King's Court's, the first English statute criminalizing sodomy was passed. . . . The common law of England, including its prohibition of sodomy, became the received law of Georgia and the other colonies. In 1816 the Georgia legislature passed the statute at issue here, and that statute has been continuously in force in one form or another since that time. To hold that the act of homosexual sodomy is somehow protected as a fundamental right would be to cast aside millennia of moral teaching. (196–97)

On and on, then, from ancient Rome through the English Reformation and the first "secular" statute condemning sodomy, until the Chief Justice approaches the Georgia Legislature's first enactment of a law against sodomy in 1816. From here, for Burger at least, it is but a day to 1986 and the upholding of that statute. (Note how Burger's condensed history—"that statute has been continuously in force *in one form or another*" [emphasis added]—conveniently skips over Georgia's 1968 revision of the sodomy law.)

But we are even more concerned with another moment that erases the complexities of history, namely, Burger's invocation of "Judaeo-Christian moral and ethical standards." The hyphen suggests an equality and even an identity between the two positions, as if any areas of difference between Judaism and Christianity are of nothing next to their shared "moral and ethical standards" around sex. In fact, whether or not "Judaism" and "Christianity" agree on questions of sexual ethics depends entirely on which Judaism and which Christianity are being considered, and even Orthodox Judaism and conservative Christianity do not agree on all issues regarding sex. Consequently, we caution against mistaking Burger's hyphenated "Judaeo-Christian" as a marker of religious pluralism in America. It seems to us, rather, that the hyphen actually passes off a wished-for assimilation of Jewish difference into Christian tradition as an instance of religious pluralism.

Additionally—and this goes to the heart of Burger's assumptions that (1) all traditions of morality are ultimately based on religion and (2) all religions agree that homosexuality is bad—when it comes time to name his sources to back up his claims, Judaism disappears from the equation. Burger cites a book entitled *Homo-sexuality and the Western Christian Tradition* as the scholarly source on which he depends for his description of this "tradition." He makes no reference to scholarship on Jewish (or other non-Christian) responses to homosexuality. Thus, he implies (all too familiarly) that Judaism is simply the "ancient roots" of a dominant Christian "tradition." On the issue of Jewish law and what Jewish traditions, in the plural, might have to say about same-sex sexual relations, Burger is stunningly silent. Judaism actually has much to say on this question; moreover, there is disagreement within Judaism over homosexuality—just as there is considerable disagreement within Christianity over homosexuality.[12] Only by bracketing real differences between Judaism and Christianity on questions of sexual ethics, not to mention real differences internal to Judaism and internal to Christianity, can Burger and others (for Burger is hardly alone in this way of thinking) so easily make opposition to "homosexual sodomy" a universal bottom line, so to speak, for morality. But isn't this logic another way of making morality over in the image of a particular interpretation of Christianity?

This strategy is visible in Burger's short history of sodomy statutes, quoted above. Let's turn back to that passage for a moment and to another particularly telling moment in it: "During the English Reformation when powers of the ecclesiastical courts were transferred to the King's Court's, the first English statute criminalizing sodomy was passed." What Burger here describes is the transcription of specifically religious laws ("ecclesiastical courts") into secular ones ("the common law of England"). By the time we get to the end of Burger's brief history of sodomy laws, these specifically religious origins are glossed over—forgotten—in the Justice's appeal to "millennia of moral teaching." With this recasting of specific religious laws as generically moral ones, the Court dispenses religion in the place of justice—and this despite the Court's responsibility to uphold the principle of church-state separation.

This is not a matter of hypocrisy or duplicity. Even as it appeals to religious doctrine the Court can truly believe that it is acting in a secular manner. How does this work? Max Weber, in his well-known study, *The Protestant Ethic and the Spirit of Capitalism,* helpfully illuminates the religious architecture of both the secular state and its free market. He reminds us that the historical developments identified with the Enlightenment—religion's retreat, reason's advance—were preceded by the Protestant Reformation. Weber draws our attention to the specific and extensive disciplines that were instituted under the name of "freedom" from the church:

> [I]t is necessary to note, what has often been forgotten, that the Reformation meant not the elimination of the Church's control over everyday life, but rather the substitution of a new form of control for the previous one. It meant the repudiation of a control which was very lax, at that time scarcely perceptible in practice and hardly more than formal, in favour of a regulation of the whole conduct which, penetrating to all departments of private and public life, was infinitely burdensome and earnestly enforced.[13]

In a historical irony, the shift of control from church to state—of which the Reformation was the beginning and which is the motor of the secularization story—has had the paradoxical effect of increasing the reach of religious authority over the body. The new disciplines of the body—a vast array of regulations, demands, expectations, ways of living the body—were more far-reaching than the Church controls that preceded them.[14]

Thus, even at its moment of institution the secular is not necessarily "free" from the religious. If the modern disciplines, or, in Weber's terms, "regulations," of the body are the site of religious authority—or, even more strongly, and still in Weber's terms, of church "control"—then when the newly secular state enforces body regulation it is also maintaining religious authority. This religious authority backs up moral claims, even without being directly named or recognized as "religious." To the extent that sexual practices have come to stand in for the body, *as the body*, then sex and sexuality will continue to present a special case, meriting special state scrutiny and moralizing concern. Certainly, *Hardwick* is an example of this maintenance of religious—Protestant—authority in the guise of secular law.

To be sure, the dissenting Justices in *Hardwick*—Blackmun, Brennan, Marshall, and Stevens—explicitly criticize the sectarian claims of Burger. Offering a spirited defense of secular values, Justice Harold Blackmun argues: "The legitimacy of secular legislation depends instead on whether the State can advance some justification for its law beyond its conformity to religious doctrine" (*Hardwick* 211). Blackmun here recognizes that religious claims are the motor behind the reasoning of the majority, and he rejects this logic. This is an important move on Blackmun's part.

Suggestively, Blackmun goes on to describe sexuality as one site for the expression of "man's spiritual nature, of his feelings and of his intellect" (207). This is a fascinating move in that, rather than appealing to religion as a basis for sexual *regulation*, Blackmun implies that sex might be an activity through which spiritual claims or values emerge. He does not further explore this possibility, which we will be taking up in the second half of this book. For now, we want to make clear that although sex is experienced by some people, perhaps by many people, as a site for spiritual expression, that does not mean that the only sex that should be free from state interference is sex that is in the service of "man's spiritual nature." We want to resist the conflation of values and religion, and we also want to clear a space for sexual practices whose value does not ultimately rest on their spiritual claims. Sometimes sex is just sex. Must sex be religion in order for it to be valued? In order for it to be legal?

Romer v. Evans

Issued ten years apart, the dispensations in *Hardwick* and *Romer* could not be more different. Or so it seems. The case that came before the Court in *Romer v. Evans* concerned the constitutionality of Colorado's Amendment 2, which a slim majority of Colorado voters had approved in a 1992 statewide referendum. Though never enforced,[15] this amendment to the Colorado state constitution would have repealed local and statewide ordinances that prohibited discrimination on the basis of "homosexual, lesbian or bisexual orientation, conduct, practices or relationships." Further, it would have prohibited the passage of any such ordinances in the future.

In a 6 to 3 ruling, the Court held that Amendment 2 was unconstitutional. Writing for the majority, and joined by Justices Ginsburg, Souter, O'Connor, Stevens, and Breyer, Justice Anthony Kennedy deftly rejected the ruse by which antidiscrimination ordinances and equal rights protections were recast as "special rights":

> We cannot accept the view that Amendment 2's prohibition on specific legal protections does no more than deprive homosexuals of special rights. To the contrary, the amendment imposes a special disability upon those persons alone. Homosexuals are forbidden the safeguards that others enjoy or may seek without constraint. . . . We find nothing special in the protections Amendment 2 withholds. These are protections taken for granted by most people either because they already have them or do not need them; these are protections against exclusion from an almost limitless number of transactions and endeavors that constitute ordinary civic life in a free society.[16]

Unable to locate "any identifiable legitimate purpose or discrete objective" for the amendment, the majority concluded that "Amendment 2 classifies homosexuals not to further a proper legislative end but to make them unequal to *everyone else"* (*Romer* 1629; emphasis added)—an "everyone else" Kennedy does not name outright, but we can infer as meaning "heterosexuals."

Although *Romer* appears to have been an unequivocal victory for gay rights, it actually produced a peculiar double bind. The majority opinion in *Romer* is thunderously silent on the case of *Hardwick,* which is nowhere mentioned in the ruling. This silence effectively sustains the state's ability to regulate bodies in their sexual acts.[17] Pitched between *Hardwick* and *Romer,* homosexuals are thus caught in the secular—and now Court-certified—version of loving the sinner while hating the sin. On the one hand, in *Romer,* the Court held that homosexuals cannot be denied the equal protection of the law simply on the basis of who they are. On the other, because *Hardwick* remains in force, "homosexual conduct" is still grounds for arrest in sixteen states.

As we have already mentioned, the identity-act or, as it is sometimes called, "status-conduct" distinction, is confused at best and contradictory at worst. Technically, the kinds of homosexual conduct that make someone liable to legal sanction in the United States are particular sexual acts. But in practice, and as we have seen with the series of events that led up to Hardwick's arrest, the category of "homosexual conduct" is much broader than sexual activity per se. In Hardwick's case, which started with the ticketing outside the gay bar, homosexual identity itself seemed to become an actionable form of homosexual practice.

This contradictory legal situation cannot be resolved simply by favoring one "side" of the identity-act distinction. The 1993 Department of Defense's policy regarding "gays in the military," for example, is also supposed to rest on a distinction between identity and acts, between homosexual status and homosexual conduct, but the policy treats the simple declaration of homosexual identity—"I am gay"— as homosexual conduct and, therefore, as sufficient grounds for discharge.[18]

When it comes to homosexuality, then, neither act nor identity provides adequate refuge from the law's reach. In a cultural scene where just saying you're gay is regarded by some as an aggressively sexual act, it is surely not enough to seek legal protections only for "being" gay. In our view, equal rights for gay people—if "equal rights" is to mean anything at all—would have to protect not just homosexual identity, but also homosexual conduct in all its rich and various forms, ranging from the right to say one is "gay," to the right to work and socialize in a "gay" bar, to the right to privacy for "homosexual" sex acts.

In contrast, then, to those who see in *Romer* a rousing victory for gay rights, we are scarcely comforted by the majority's failure to address "homosexual conduct." The minority showed no such compunction. Indeed, the dissent never ceases to address "homosexual conduct." The dissenting Justices' energetic defense of Amendment 2 even depends upon it. They seek to make *Hardwick* and the body regulation it licenses the constitutional shelter for Amendment 2's more expansive reach.

As will become clear below, we do not agree with the minority's reasoning. At the same time, however, we do think there is an unresolved and potentially dangerous tension between *Romer* and *Hardwick*. The minority opinion in *Romer* starkly showcases this tension, which is among the reasons that we now focus our attention upon the dissent. We are concerned that *Hardwick* and the type of regulations it represents can continue to constrain not just sexual activity but equal participation in civic life. This concern is amplified by the fact that the makeup of the Supreme Court is in no way stable. Certainly, the sexual conservatism of the current administration does not leave us optimistic about the future course the Court might take.

In a scathing dissent, to which Chief Justice Rehnquist and Justice Thomas also signed their names, Justice Antonin Scalia called the majority in *Romer* to account for ignoring the Court's own legal precedents. Had the majority only consulted the Court's recent past, he writes, it would have found the "legitimate rational basis for the substance of the amendment." He continues:

In *Bowers v. Hardwick,* . . . we held that the Constitution does not prohibit what virtually all States had done from the founding of the Republic until very recent years—making homosexual conduct a crime. That holding is unassailable, except by those who think that the Constitution changes to suit current fashion. . . . If it is constitutionally permissible for a State to make homosexual conduct criminal [as *Hardwick* held], surely it is constitutionally permissible for a State to enact other laws merely *disfavoring* homosexual conduct. (1631; emphasis in original)

To Scalia, homosexuality *is* its conduct. Over the course of his opinion, homosexual conduct becomes a disturbingly elastic category, expanding to include not just sexual but political activity.

In the short passage above, Scalia makes three references to "homosexual conduct." In the first two instances, he is clearly referring to *Hardwick* and thus to "homosexual sodomy"—although he does not use this term. By the time Scalia arrives at his third and final mention of "homosexual conduct," however, he is no longer discussing *Hardwick;* he is discussing the case before the Court in 1996, *Romer.* In this shift from *Hardwick* to *Romer* he also makes a rhetorical bait and switch: from sex to political activity. *Romer* is not about sex acts, but about the political act of advocating and passing gay rights legislation. Scalia's entire argument depends upon a slippage between homosexual conduct as sex and homosexual conduct as anything that a homosexual might do on behalf of homosexuals, up to and including advocating gay rights.

We can see this slippage again in a later passage when he differentiates between giving favored status to people who happen to be homosexual (which he says Amendment 2 would still permit) and giving them this favored status because of homosexual "conduct." People who are homosexual might be favored insofar as they also happen to be people who are "senior citizens or members of racial minorities," he argues (1633). So, for example, the actions of a gay person who is organizing and petitioning on behalf of the American Association of Retired Persons would remain recognized and protected political activities. By contrast, under the terms of Amendment 2—terms that Scalia and the other two dissenting Justices voted to uphold—if that same gay person wanted to leaflet, organize, and petition on behalf of gay rights, his or her activity could have no legislative result.

Scalia's logic is not simply flawed; it has perilous consequences for democracy in the United States. What's at issue in Amendment 2 is antidiscrimination laws that were achieved through regular democratic processes. It is not just that Amendment 2 would have overturned existing gay rights ordinances in Colorado; it would have blocked gay rights advocates, whether or not they were homosexual, from restoring these antidiscrimination laws or passing any new ones. Scalia is at pains to characterize Amendment 2 as democracy at work, calling Amendment 2 "a modest attempt by seemingly tolerant Coloradans to preserve traditional sexual mores against the efforts of a politically powerful minority to revise those mores through law" (1629). But in fact Amendment 2 was an attempt to preempt equal participation in U.S. democracy.

Scalia does not see things this way. Homosexuals (and their allies?) do not seem to be part of the American political project as he imagines it. They certainly are not part of his fantasy "public at large":

The problem (a problem, that is, for those who wish to retain social disapprobation of homosexuality) is that, because those who engage in homosexual conduct tend to reside in disproportionate numbers in certain communities, . . . have high disposable income, . . . and of course care about homosexual-rights issues more ardently than the public at large, they possess political power greater than their numbers, both locally and statewide. (1634)

We want to look at the work that the "public at large" does for Scalia. Its invocation marks the boundaries of "us" and "them," helping to construct a middle ground, a place of "tolerance." However, this promised tolerance does not go very far. The ultimate problem with homosexuals, in Scalia's accounting, is that "Quite understandably, they devote [their disproportionate] political power to achieving not merely a grudging social toleration, but full social acceptance, of homosexuality" (1634). In Scalia's rhetorical balancing act, homosexuals are not members of the group that extends tolerance, but only the potential objects of that proffered—and finely measured—tolerance. They are certainly not equal citizens—and this despite the fact that they supposedly have such excessive political capital at their disposal.

Scalia establishes the disproportion of this putative homosexual political power by borrowing a series of anti-Semitic tropes that insinuate greedy self-interest. This rhetorical borrowing effects a substitution (in no way an innocent or recent one) of "homosexual" for "Jew."[19] Indeed, these ominous images of self-interested persons, who are greedy for income, greedy for real estate, and greedy for political influence, can be found in any number of historic anti-Semitic tracts.[20] As Scalia's anxious series of images unfolds, piling danger upon danger (but for whom exactly?), political activity on behalf of gay rights actually turns out to be one of the forms of homosexual conduct that the "public at large" has every reason to resent and every right to curtail.

In our view, the anti-Semitic resonances of Scalia's rhetoric are not incidental features of his argument. At base, the "public at large," whose rights to free association Scalia would protect from homosexual interference, is implicitly Christian. His commendation of "tolerant Coloradans," who are just trying "to preserve traditional sexual mores" (1629), reiterates the Christian assumptions that were stated more openly by the majority in *Hardwick*. That is, where Justice Burger cites "Judaeo-Christian moral and ethical standards" (even though, in the end, Burger is only talking about *Christian* standards), Scalia refers, more obliquely but no less insidiously, to "traditional sexual mores." Given Scalia's approving citation of *Hardwick* and given too the anti-Semitic tropes that energize his argument, what can "traditional" mean in this context but "Christian"? (So much for the "Judaeo" in "Judaeo-Christian.")

Indeed, it is hard to resist the notion that the anti-Semitic recoding of homosexuality is where Scalia was heading all along; the first line of his dissent is "The Court has mistaken a Kulturkampf for a fit of spite" (1629). It is difficult to hear the word "Kulturkampf" (literally, "culture conflict") without hearing in it an echo of nineteenth- and early twentieth-century German debates about whether or not Catholics and Jews were "real" Germans. We want to be very clear on this point: we are not here accusing the Justice of deliberate anti-Semitism. Scalia's intentions—whether he chose these images knowingly or not—are not the point. Rather, he is speaking out of a shared—and largely unconscious—cultural logic. This cultural logic depends upon the establishment of an exclusionary notion of Americanness. Within its terms, antigay discrimination is reasonable precisely because homosexuals can be constructed out of the meaning of America—as Jews once were and perhaps still are (invocations of "Judaeo-Christian" values notwithstanding).

In the end, for Scalia the "traditional" moral condemnation of homosexuality is strong enough that it is constitutionally acceptable to curtail the political activity of not just homosexuals but anyone who would advocate gay rights. Not only are the "traditional sexual mores" Scalia defends ultimately those of the Christian tradition, but their defense is undertaken in terms that have historically been used to enforce Christian dominance in the United States.

What is particularly surprising is how easily domination can be undertaken in the name of tolerance. Certainly, the language of tolerance that peppers Scalia's dissent does not counteract but actually carries forward this logic of exclusion. The "degree of hostility reflected by Amendment 2 is," we learn, "the smallest conceivable" (1633). Scalia conserves the Americanness of opposition to homosexuality:

"The Court's opinion contains grim, disapproving hints that Coloradans have been guilty of 'animus' or 'animosity' toward homosexuality, as though that has been established as Unamerican" (1633). He takes for granted "our moral heritage that one should not hate any human being or class of human beings" (1633). But this putatively shared "moral heritage" notwithstanding, Scalia goes on to list "certain conduct" it is reasonable to consider "reprehensible": "murder, for example, or polygamy, or cruelty to animals," and he concludes that "one [and note the impersonal disembodied 'one'] could exhibit even 'animus' toward such conduct" (1633). It is this and only this—morally justified "animus" toward homosexuality—that Scalia claims Amendment 2 enacts.

Consider the odd inversion and, then, substitutions of Scalia's rhetoric: "The Court has mistaken a Kulturkampf for a fit of spite." Not only does he deny that Amendment 2 represents unwarranted "animus," but he also effectively shifts the agents of Kulturkampf from the presumptively heterosexual electoral majority who approved Amendment 2 to homosexuals—and their allies on the Court. By Scalia's own reasoning, then, the Kulturkampf is one initiated and carried out by homosexuals whose single-minded pursuit of homosexual rights does not stop at achieving "grudging social toleration," but aims at nothing short of "full social acceptance" (1634). The majority in *Romer* gets aligned with this homosexual "minority," which is supposedly seeking to impose its will on the "public at large." Thus Scalia: "This court has no business imposing upon all Americans the resolution favored by the elite class from which the members of this institution are selected" (1634).

This rhetorical flourish does more than simply set up a binary between "all Americans" and the six Supreme Court Justices who voted to declare Amendment 2 unconstitutional. It also equates the slim majority of Colorado voters who supported Amendment 2 at the polls with "all Americans"—as if it would be "Unamerican" not to endorse the Amendment's exclusionary views. Finally, once this series of substitutions is in place, Scalia's new balance sheet effectively repositions those who would exclude gay men, lesbians, and bisexuals from American democracy as the ones most in need of legal protection. In other words, the people (Scalia's phantom "public at large") whose rights are already recognized and enforced are the ones treated as if their rights were endangered. By contrast, the very people who face discrimination and even danger in their everyday lives would be actively excluded from political redress under Scalia's reasoning. This is the lie of "special rights," and tolerance is its alibi.

It is vital to underscore this point: Scalia's entire argument takes place under the terms of tolerance, not hate. Accusing homosexuals (and other historically marginalized groups) of overreaching provides a smokescreen behind which fundamentally exclusionary practices can be repackaged as "modest" and "tolerant." But Justice Scalia is not just speaking for himself and the other two dissenters. Rather, his legal arguments reflect a larger cultural logic that shapes public debates about homosexuality and gay rights in the United States. This is why the dissent in *Romer* must be taken so seriously; the views expressed in it are not in any simple sense "minority" perspectives.

Ultimately, if *Romer* is a victory for gay rights, it is a limited one. It is limited on both sides by tolerance. The majority opinion provides no relief from *Hardwick* and the restrictions on sexual life it licenses. Thus, the tolerance that the majority in *Romer* extends to homosexual persons does not include freedom for sexual practice. For the dissenters, tolerance is on the side of those Coloradans who only want to "retain social disapprobation of homosexuality." But in either case, in both the majority and minority opinions, tolerance sanctions the cutting off of body from person—and sin from sinner.

In *Hardwick* the Court explicitly draws on religion to enforce the regulation of "homosexual sodomy." The Court can sustain such an apparently blatant violation of the separation of church and state because it has collapsed the complex history of relations among religion, secular morality, bodily regulation, and sexual regulation. The effect of religiously derived sexual regulation in *Hardwick* is extremely important to trace because the majority opinion in *Romer* appears to protect homosexual identity. Homosexuals' participation in what Justice Kennedy calls "ordinary civic life" is protected, even as Kennedy's majority decision lets stand the regulation of homosexual conduct. Evidently, the "almost limitless number of transactions and endeavors that constitute[s] ordinary civic life in a free society" meets its limit at sexual practice.

Romer's three-man minority is all too willing to conflate the sexual regulation endorsed by *Hardwick* with the regulation of nonsexual homosexual, or even homosexual-friendly, activity. In other words, the dissenting Justices are utterly willing to regulate identity, and not "just" practice. We cannot simply dismiss the minority's opinion and rest easy that, at the end of the day, Amendment 2's unconstitutionality was affirmed. Scalia's dissent, even though it was the "losing" perspective, nevertheless suggests the staying power of Christian dominance in U.S. public life. Finally, then, the issue boils down to this: the distinction between the result in *Hardwick* and the result in *Romer* rests upon the distinction between act and identity, sin and sinner. In practice, this sin-sinner distinction is no distinction at all.

2 What's Wrong with Tolerance?

"Love the sinner and hate the sin" is an inadequate formulation for dealing with the politics of sexuality. The line between whom we are supposed to love (the sinner) and what we are supposed to hate (the sin) is impossibly movable and contradictory. Just as problematic, this love-hate relation produces tolerance, rather than freedom and justice, as the major way of understanding a range of differences in the United States. This is not just a question of sexuality. Tolerance is supposed to be a sign of openness and a wedge against hate; but in practice it is exclusionary, hierarchical, and ultimately nondemocratic. Tolerance is certainly an improvement over hate, but it is not the same thing as freedom. Paradoxically, tolerance is at once un-American and the most American thing of all.

The history of tolerance in the United States, like the history of sexual regulation, is inseparable from the history of religion. Concepts of religious tolerance—or toleration—were developed in Europe in response to the "wars of religion" that were sparked by the Protestant Reformation. European Christianity was no longer dominated by one "holy, catholic, and apostolic" church, but by several different religions laying claim, sometimes violently, to the title of "true religion." This was also the period of state formation, in which various forms of social amalgamation—fiefdoms, princely estates, and commonweals—gradually became what we know of today as nation-states. The shifts in social configuration from the sixteenth through the nineteenth centuries that made modern nation-states were themselves often violent.

Most conventional histories of the Reformation and its aftermath understand the "wars of religion" to have been resolved through the development of religious tolerance. But this tolerance, from its inception, was quite limited. For example, in England, the Established Church was (and remains) a Protestant church, the Church of England. The "Toleration Act" of 1689 removed certain legal penalties against those Protestants who dissented from the Church of England, and it ended the requirement that all British subjects subscribe to the articles of faith of the Church of England. Crucially, however, the Act did not protect non-Protestant dissenters from persecution. Catholics and Jews, Muslims and atheists, were all outside the bounds of official tolerance. Although the boundaries of toleration have been expanded over time, the Church of England remains the established and official faith of England.

The limits of the Toleration Act were not just its narrow boundaries, but the social hierarchy it established and reaffirmed. As historian Justin Champion points out, "[the Toleration Act] did not break the link between civic liberties and religious identity. So, for example, while Quakers were no longer in danger of eradication by persecution (as long as they registered as non-conformists), they were still exempt from holding local, civic or national offices which were still protected by statutory tests of conscience."[1] In other words, the civic peace that religious tolerance was supposed to achieve institutes a hierarchy. After all, being allowed to live in peace (being "no longer in danger of eradication"), and being a free and equal member of society are two different things. The Toleration Act allowed people who practiced other faiths (or no faith at all) to "exist," but they could not claim the same rights and privileges as members of the Church of England. Toleration, then, falls well short of democratic equality.

The American principles of religious freedom were supposed to overcome these limits of toleration. In principle, religious freedom provides for the equal treatment of different faiths—there is no established church, and all religions are free to practice as they please. But this ideal of religious freedom has never really been enacted in the United States. On matters of religion, the United States has two conflicting self-understandings: that this is a nation of religious freedom and equality, and that this is a basically Christian nation. Thus, in practice, life in the United States has proven to be much more like the situation in Britain than our national mythology implies. If tolerance marks a space of well-defined hierarchy like that between the Church of England and other religious faiths in Britain, what is the place of tolerance in a society that is supposedly based on the free and equal participation of all citizens?

These tensions between religious difference and the claims of tolerance were foundational to the emergence of the United States. Not only did colonists like William Penn come to the Americas seeking sanctuary for religious differences, but they also imposed a particular understanding of religious difference on those around them. Despite the fact that Penn established Pennsylvania on the basis of religious tolerance in 1682, seven years before the British Act of Toleration, he too offered only a narrow version of tolerance—one in which only Christian men could vote. In the American colonies as well, religious toleration was only offered to various versions of Christianity (sometimes failing to include Catholics); toleration did not apply to those who were not Christian, most notably American Indians and non-Christian Africans.

Thus, in America as well as in Britain, the initial boundaries of tolerance were narrow and offered only to differences *within* Christianity. Those who were Christian in a nondominant way (who were, for example, Catholic) might be tolerated, if marginalized, but at least they were no longer, as Champion so succinctly put it, "in danger of eradication." But there were others who were not Christian and, hence, remained outside the bounds of tolerance. These "others" could be eradicated, as was so often the case in Christian interactions with American Indians, or enslaved, as was the case with Africans.

In fact, as a number of historians have noted, the original distinction that determined who could be enslaved in the colonies and who could not was not a racial distinction, but a distinction between "Christians and strangers."[2] In her research, religious studies scholar Emilie Townes has discovered that as late as 1753 the law codes of the colony of Virginia relied upon the language of religious identity, not race, to define slavery, even though slavery had for some time been "based on racial, not religious difference."[3] Indentured servants who were "Christian" might work off their indenture over some fixed period of time and become free. Slaves, on the other hand, could never work their way to freedom; it could only be granted by their "masters."

In all this, the category of "Christian" anticipates future categories of race and national identity. Before the nationalist distinction between British and American citizens that was forged in the American Revolution, the white British colonists were simply "Christians." To put the point more strongly, the category "white" was not yet fully operative.

As we can see from these few examples, identity categories that seem so self-evident and so natural to us today are and have been contingent, changeable, and confused. In U.S. history this confusion was intensified by the fact that Christianity is a missionary religion, and thus many Native Americans and some Africans were converted to Christianity. Historian John Sweet has argued that this complication, which resulted when "strangers" became "Christians," was one of the driving forces behind the institutionalization of racial categories in the colonies and, later, the United States.[4] Eventually, a (secularized) racial distinction, rather than a religious one, came to define those who were outside the community—those who could be eradicated or enslaved.

This history teaches us that in the United States religious understandings of difference have served as the basis upon which secular social differences (for example, race and ethnicity) have been constructed. It is not that religious distinctions have disappeared or are inoperative in American life, but that they have sometimes been absorbed into other social differences, such as those that define racial, national, and ethnic identity. Contemporary conflations of Arabs with Muslims, for example, show how confusion between religious and ethnic or national identities persists. Similarly, "tolerance" emerges out of a specifically religious history that may not be directly named, but that remains powerful. Thus, as we argued in the first chapter, Protestantism is expressed in American secular sexual regulation, and so too have Protestant understandings of religious tolerance influenced areas of our social life that now seem fully secular.

To be sure, the boundaries of tolerance have expanded; Jews, Muslims, and even atheists are included within the circle of those who are to be tolerated in America. Nonetheless, the basic structures of difference and hierarchy established by religious tolerance continue powerfully to affect American social relations. There are still those in America who are central and those who are marginal, but tolerated. One can technically be a citizen and yet not be treated as a full member of American society, and the dangers are redoubled for those who are not citizens but are placed in categories like "resident alien" and "illegal alien." After the terrible events of September 11, 2001, we saw how quickly those who are the objects of tolerance can be singled out, as Muslims or those who were perceived to be Muslims were questioned, detained, and surveilled by the government (whether or not they were U.S. citizens). In the immediate aftermath of September 11, some men were even killed in acts of vigilante violence directed at Muslims. The perpetrators of these vigilante acts understood themselves to be acting as patriots, in defense of the nation.

It can be quite dangerous to be offered tolerance rather than full membership in American public life.

As was the case with the "wars of religion," tolerance is often advocated as the response to this type of hateful, eradicating violence. However, in our view, contemporary secularized tolerance is as inadequate a response to hatred and violence as was (and is) religious tolerance. Freedom and equality, rather than tolerance and hierarchy, are the appropriate response to social differences in a democratic society.

It is sometimes difficult to see what's wrong with tolerance because tolerance is so often invoked as the best response to discrimination and hatred. Even groups like the Southern Poverty Law Center, the organization perhaps most responsible for bringing hate groups to justice, advocate that we "teach tolerance" in order to battle hatred.

However, tolerance doesn't really fight the problem of hatred; it maintains the very structures of hierarchy and discrimination on which hatred is based. This is a highly counterintuitive claim. As we have just suggested in our discussion of religious toleration, tolerance establishes a hierarchical relation between a dominant center and its margins. Another way to put this is to say that tolerance sets up an us-them relation in which "we" tolerate "them."

How different is this from hate? Not unlike tolerance, hate crimes also take the form of an us-them relation—an "us" who must violently eradicate a "them." The perpetrator often understands this violent eradication as an act of defense, not aggression. He (and less frequently, she) is only acting to protect himself or his community or his values from those "outsiders" who threaten all that he holds dear.

Let us return for a moment to our discussion of Supreme Court Justice Antonin Scalia's dissent in *Romer v. Evans*. In his dissent Scalia refers repeatedly to a "public at large." In a country based on freedom and equality, this "public at large" should

refer to all Americans. However, when Scalia refers to "all Americans," he effectively excludes some people from this category: homosexuals and the "cultural
elite," whose views, he asserts, were articulated by the six Supreme Court Justices
who held Colorado's Amendment 2 to be unconstitutional. Scalia's "public at
large" is exclusionary, not expansive; it constructs an "us" that specifically leaves
out a particular "them"—in this instance, homosexuals and their allies.

This is not just a question of conservative Supreme Court Justices. The rhetorical practices through which a narrow segment of the American public is represented as "all" of it are repeated, often unthinkingly, across a wide range of contexts. For example, when the mainstream media reported on AIDS in the early
years of the pandemic, they would ask questions like, "Is AIDS a threat to the general public?" Now, if the "general public" includes everyone, this question would
be meaningless; that some people in the United States—some members of the public—already had AIDS was not in dispute. AIDS was (and remains) a threat to Americans, and hence the question, is AIDS a threat to the general public, is effectively
tautological. However, the reason this could be a meaningful question was because
the "general public" did not really include everybody; it did not include those persons who had been identified as members of "at-risk" groups, such as homosexuals, hemophiliacs, and intravenous drug users.

One of the ways that widespread empathy for people with AIDS developed was
through images of "innocent victims," hemophiliacs such as Ryan White, who
could simultaneously be one of us (a representative American) and one of them (a
member of an "at-risk" group). But unlike hemophiliacs, homosexuals and intravenous drug users were not so easily moved from the category of "them" to "us."
These Americans were not considered part of the general American public; indeed,
they, rather than HIV, were sometimes even seen as a threat to "us."

Whenever "we" are asked to tolerate those "others," this same center-mar-
gins relationship comes into play. If "Americans" are asked to tolerate "homosexuals," it means that at some level homosexuals are not fully Americans. Being

the object of tolerance does not represent full inclusion in American life, but rather a grudging form of acceptance in which the boundary between "us" and "them" remains clear, sometimes dangerously so. This boundary is also elevated to a mark of moral virtue. The tolerant are generous and open-minded even as they are exclusionary. How can a tolerance that depends on defining someone as an outsider be the opposite of hate? To teach tolerance is to teach precisely the type of us-them relationship upon which hate thrives. Teaching tolerance, then, cannot be the answer to hate and excessive violence, nor can tolerance adequately address other forms of social division.

To get a better sense of the mechanisms through which tolerance creates an exclusionary, rather than democratic, public, we want to analyze the media coverage of a series of murders committed in recent years. We turn first to the tragic murder of gay college student Matthew Shepard, who was beaten, tied to a fence, and left for dead in Laramie, Wyoming, in October 1998. Next, we look at the case of Dr. Barnett Slepian, who was shot to death later that same fall, in November 1998. James Kopp, the man charged with murdering Slepian, is affiliated with the Army of God, a radical antiabortion group. Evidently, Slepian was killed because he provided abortions as part of his medical practice in Buffalo, New York. We go on to consider two police shootings that involved excessive violence: the December 28, 1998 shooting of Tyisha Miller, a young African American woman in California, and the killing in early February 1999 of Amadou Diallo, an immigrant to New York City from Guinea, West Africa. Only one of these deaths was named a "hate crime" (Shepard's). Yet the killings of Slepian, Miller, and Diallo also reflect basic social divisions in America. In examining the media coverage of all four of these killings, we seek to explore how public understandings of difference and belonging in America are framed and organized.

The media—both print and television—occupy an especially privileged place in American public life. The way they represent new or apparently new phenomena (because crimes motivated by prejudice are hardly new to the American scene) profoundly affects how such events are understood. The media do not just neutrally report what they see; they also help to determine what can be seen, what can be represented. The media, that is, act as filters, grids of cultural intelligibility. At the same time, it is not as if the media deliberately present a distorted picture of the world. The mainstream media are not somehow apart from the larger American imaginary, but emerge out of it. Thus, how the media discuss violence and social division is less a matter of good (or bad) intentions than it is of reflexively repeating longer-standing assumptions about who and what constitutes the American middle ground.

It is both interesting and surprising that public narratives produced in response to extreme acts should so often reiterate and unintentionally reinforce existing social divisions. We can see something of this pattern in the way the mainstream media represented Matthew Shepard's murder. Shepard's death produced a remarkable moment in which it seemed that the majority of Americans, who had ignored so many gay-bashings and antigay murders in the past, were for the first time expressing real sympathy for the plight of gay men and lesbians. And yet, alongside the hand wringing and soul-searching, the discomforting ambivalences of tolerance remained.

Time, for example, featured the Shepard story on its cover (October 26, 1998), as did most of the major news magazines. *Time*'s cover displayed a blown-up image of the deer fence to which Matthew Shepard's two assailants tied him and left him for dead. A small photo of a smiling Shepard was cut into the lower left side of the cover (Figure 1). The two images were powerful in their juxtaposition, but their power and poignancy were undercut by the caption: "The War Over Gays." We might have expected *Time* to write, "The War *On* Gays" rather than "The War *Over* Gays." This is not an idle difference. Between the prepositions "on" and "over" there is a world of difference—an American landscape divided, again, between "us" and "them."[5]

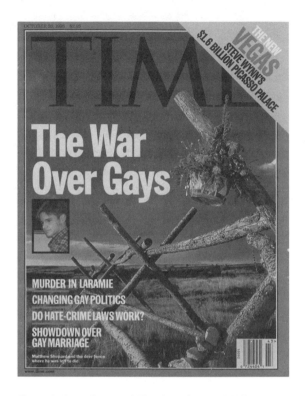

Figure 1. Cover image of *Time* (October 26, 1998).

Time assumes an audience of readers made up of middle America, the "general public." How might the language of "The War On Gays" have resonated, and resonated differently? If the murder of Matthew Shepard were represented as a "war *on* gays," then *Time*'s idealized readership—John and Jane Q. Public—would be implicated in this "war." The readers would have been challenged to confront the realities of extreme prejudice and inequality and recognize that some Americans are singled out, targeted even unto death, just for who they are. More starkly, the language of "The War On Gays" would have pressed *Time*'s readers to consider on which side of the fence they stood: with the objects of hate or with its agents.

However, in the end *Time* could not name the type of violence faced by gays and lesbians in the United States as a "war on gays." Instead middle America was rhetorically excused from having to take a stand. Even more strongly, we could say that the caption "The War Over Gays" exempts "ordinary" Americans from any responsibility for hatred or violence. The implied participants in the "war" over gays are, on one "side," those who refuse to tolerate homosexuals, who would deny gay persons basic American rights (including the right to life), and on the other "side," homosexuals themselves, particularly those who are perceived as activists for gay rights.

As presented by *Time,* the combatants in the "war" are those who hate and fight against gays and those who fight back against this hatred. Notably absent or at least removed to a safe distance from this opposition between those who hate and those who are hated is *Time*'s idealized average, ordinary, and tolerant American. Strikingly, then, to be hated can place you in the same position as those who hate. If you fight back against that hate (particularly if you organize with others against hatred) you too become a combatant in the "war." You are no longer "innocent," you are an agitator, a crusader, a fighter, and, as such, you fall outside the boundaries of the American "general public." In this "war," the only innocents are those who stand to the side—outside, above, or "over" the fray. If the problem of murderous violence is not taken to be injustice (that we as a society subordinate entire groups of people), but is instead categorized as extremism (that our social relations have turned into all-out combat), then within the terms of this formulation those who are the objects of violence are located at one of the extremes, a position distinct from the middle.

In the same year that Matthew Shepard was killed, there were 2,574 antigay assaults.[6] In the face of this we must ask why this particular murder touched a chord in American public life. Like Ryan White before him, Matthew Shephard could be assimilated into the dream of "normal" America. News reports referred to him as "anyone's son." He was a blond middle- to upper-middle-class young man, he was reportedly shy and somewhat reserved, and, although he attended meetings of the gay student group at the University of Wyoming, he was not particularly politically active on behalf of gay rights. He was in many respects an ordinary college student. Of course, not just "anyone's son" goes to college. Attending college is both a benchmark of economic arrival and a signature of middle-class identity in America; many people were able to identify with Shepard and with his parents because he so closely matched this profile. But this picture of Matthew Shepard as an ordinary American allowed him to be seen as an innocent bystander in the polarized "war" over gays. He could become part of the tolerant middle. Although many Americans were apparently willing to bring Matthew Shepard into this middle, *Time* could not allow "gays" as a group to reside there.

This dynamic is a three-part interaction in which a pair of opposites, those who hate and those who are hated, flank a third party, the tolerant middle. The tolerant middle is rarely named directly; it doesn't have to be. This phantom called "middle America" is both the assumed audience and the assumed subject of public address.

We can see these assumptions at work in the media coverage of Dr. Barnett Slepian's 1998 murder. On November 15, 1998, the *New York Times* published an article about the killing entitled "Stubborn Belief in Duty Guided Slain Doctor, Friends Say He Performed Abortions from Principle, Not as a Crusader." The article opened as follows:

> To his tormentors, he was simply an abortion doctor. To members of the abortion rights movement, he was a martyr for the cause. But Dr. Slepian was far from either. He was killed because he performed a medical procedure that has become emotional and politicized. Yet there is nothing in his life to suggest he was a crusader in either politics or medicine.

Unlike the murder of Matthew Shepard, Dr. Slepian's murder was not called a "hate crime." But what does the *Times*'s coverage of Slepian's murder tell us about American understandings of violence and social division?

On one level the *Times* is simply saying that Dr. Slepian was providing a medical procedure that the Supreme Court has said is available on the basis of a constitutionally protected right to privacy. Certainly, medical service provision should not require risking one's life. And yet, we must ask, why did Dr. Slepian's medical practice lead to his murder? It is not just because the practice had become "emotional and politicized," but because this particular procedure—abortion—has to do with women and with women's rights specifically. Once again, what is at issue is a basic social division and hierarchy in our society: that of gender. But the *Times* does not mention gender hierarchy or women's rights at all. Rather, the problem as presented by the *Times* is one of emotion and politicization—in short, of extremism.

Dr. Slepian is represented as an innocent bystander in this particular "war," and those who fight to protect women's rights are implicitly set up on one extreme, with those who use murderous violence positioned on the other. The *Times* is at great pains to extract Slepian from the politics of abortion. Unlike abortion rights' advocates or opponents of abortion rights, Slepian was neither overly emotional nor political about what he was doing. No crusader, he was just a man doing his job. *Times*'s characterization of the way these two "sides" mistakenly viewed Slepian ("simply an abortion doctor" versus "a martyr for the cause") ultimately suggests there is nothing really to distinguish the two extremes (opponents and advocates of abortion rights) from each other.

What does this imply about members of the abortion rights movement? Are those who work politically to protect women's rights different from Slepian and from the general public? Interestingly, the *Times*'s characterization puts women, or at least women's rights, in a minority position, despite the fact that women themselves are statistically in the majority. One of the effects of this structure in

American politics is the consistent construction of "minorities." Those on either side of this political conflict are implicitly understood to be taking minority viewpoints through which abortion becomes "emotional" or "politicized." In contrast, those involved in the medical provision of abortion services are positioned as outside this debate—as long as they are not crusaders. Here the *Times* is participating in the construction of the general public. What does it mean for a democratic society that this general public is delineated in such a way that it does not include anyone who can be identified as a "crusader," whether for or against abortion rights? Are we thus left without analytic tools for distinguishing between political advocacy ("politicization") and murderous violence?

Not only does tolerance reinforce structural inequality, but it also sets up a political culture in which extremism, rather than injustice, is the major problem to be addressed in public life. In a public organized around tolerance, the question is not whether we as a society have created unjust (and violent) social hierarchies, but whether we as individuals hate anyone. This disabling structure of tolerance has important implications for participatory democracy because it puts those who take up political activism in any form at risk for charges of extremism.

Because the tolerant middle must be distinguished from both sides of any political conflict, the "violence" of our social life can be projected onto either side of a political debate regardless of the specifics of the situation. A very clear example is provided by historian Karen Anderson's study of school integration in Little Rock, Arkansas. The Little Rock schools were the first of the segregated schools to be integrated through court order on the basis of *Brown v. Board of Education* (1954). As Anderson documents, the self-proclaimed "moderates" in Little Rock saw the problem as one of extremism on "both sides," meaning the white majority that defended segregation and the predominantly African American minority that advocated for integration. Note how this "two sides to every story" approach makes each side appear to be equally problematic whatever their differences. The moderates' vision of extremism was one with which President Eisenhower agreed, and there was significant police and military presence surrounding the high school on the first day of classes. This show of state force was brought out to prevent "violence"—violence directed against the nine black students who were the first African Americans to attend Little Rock High School, yes, but also violence that the "white community" feared from the black students and their supporters.[7]

These students were assumed to be potentially violent because they were violating the long-standing codes of conduct under segregation and because they were opposed by violent forces. There was no indication from the students or the African American community of Little Rock that they would be the source of violence. In fact, given how greatly they were outnumbered, it would have been foolhardy (if not suicidal) for any of the students to have incited violence. Yet the government treated "both sides" as if they were equally likely to become violent.

In a situation framed by the rhetoric of tolerance, it becomes impossible to distinguish between the perpetrators of racism or homophobia or misogyny (this list is hardly exhaustive) and the objects of various forms of discrimination. Rather, when the situation is characterized by tolerance, the public is not expected to take a stand against injustice, but merely to tolerate both sides of a conflict. In fact, the public can become paralyzed in its ability to address injustice, because it cannot distinguish between competing claims and groups that it is supposed to tolerate.

More seriously, this paralysis can lead to other category confusions. In the debates over "hate crimes" laws in Wyoming that followed Matthew Shepard's murder, there were those who claimed that, as one woman stated directly, Wyoming was the "real victim of bias crime."[8] Here is a typical reversal, which can only make sense if we buy into the assumption that both sides of a social conflict are extremists. If each side is as bad as the other, it is impossible to distinguish between them. The woman who made this comment is at one level simply saying that the media coverage of Wyoming in the wake of the Matthew Shepard killing had been biased.

This is true, in part, given the northeastern and urban biases of much of the mainstream media.[9]

But on another level this claim is given its rhetorical punch by equating media coverage of a crime with that crime and, specifically, with the crime of murder. While we take media representations seriously, they are not the same thing as physical violence, nor is biased reporting a crime like murder. If the "real" hate crime is committed against Wyoming because the state is characterized as harboring a homophobia that produces murderous violence, then, as in the Little Rock example, it becomes impossible to distinguish between the perpetrators of murderous violence and those who are its victims. The idea that any bias is as extreme and as bad as any other makes it impossible to distinguish between perpetrators and victims of injustice.

Framing our public discussions in terms of tolerance versus hate makes it seem as though the major problem we confront as a nation is one of misplaced feelings rather than problematic social relations. Tolerance is supposed to remedy a specific feeling (hate) or disposition (bias). This form of response personalizes and decontextualizes a larger issue, disconnecting feelings or biases from both structures of power and the everyday enactments of those power relations.

If hate crimes seem so inexplicable, this is in part because the vast majority of people in the United States do not experience themselves as hating anyone. They are not openly racist or sexist or homophobic, but neither do they embrace the victims of hate. Here is the crucial point. We are not suggesting that there is no difference between the majority of tolerant Americans and those few who commit murderous violence. That difference is utterly important. However, we are suggesting that a tolerant stance does not allow Americans to act effectively against hatred and murderous violence. If the "war" is "over" gays, rather than "on" gays, and both "sides" are placed on the extremes and apart from the "general public," then we cannot make an effective distinction between those who hate and those who are the victims of hate. Tolerance does not allow us to address the injustices that make some persons the likely objects of murderous violence.

To embrace the victims of hate does not mean, however, that all Americans must agree about the moral status of homosexuality. If we were to move outside the framework of tolerance to a framework of freedom, we would be able to stand up for the victims of homophobic violence whether or not we thought homosexuality was a sin. It would be possible for those who believed that homosexuality is a sin to embrace the religious freedom of those who thought otherwise. This stance is not the tolerance of loving the sinner and hating the sin. It is the democracy of religious freedom in which one group's idea of sin does not limit the freedom of those who believe and practice differently, in which laws are based on democratic processes, not on particular religious beliefs. The majority of Americans do not hate anyone, but neither do they grant the same democratic freedoms to everyone.

Surprisingly, even those who commit hate crimes do not experience themselves as hateful people. A recent study by forensic psychologist Karen Franklin of youths who admit to harassing or bashing gay men found that the youths understand themselves to be enforcing moral values.[10] Similarly, historian Kathleen Blee has interviewed women who participate in organizations that would commonly be called "hate groups."[11] These women understand their groups not to be about hate, but to be concerned with positive values that maintain tradition and culture. Focusing on "hate," therefore, will not tell us very much about those who are generally perceived to be hateful.

What leads to violence, then, is not some simple expression of hatred. More often it is a sense of threat, the feeling, for example, of the women interviewed by Blee that their traditions were being threatened. This sense of threat is a crucially important factor in many of the crimes that have now been labeled "hate." In the murder of Matthew Shepard, for example, representatives of the perpetrators repeatedly denied that it was a hate crime. There were certainly concrete reasons for making this claim. The two young men were initially charged with a capital crime and faced the death penalty. Thus, the defendants had an interest in avoiding any appearance of extreme malice and forethought that might make a jury more likely to impose the death sentence.

But we can also learn something if we take seriously the claim that the two perpetrators were not simply motivated by hate. For example, in an October 14, 1998 interview for the television news program "20/20," reporter John Quiñones asked Kristen Price, the girlfriend of one of the perpetrators, Aaron McKinney, whether the killing was a hate crime. She denied it, saying that this interpretation was being imposed on the situation. Quiñones followed up by asking why McKinney and the other perpetrator, Russell Henderson, had beaten Matthew Shepard so brutally if robbery were the only motive. Price's response in the end came down to a single word, "Humiliation." She explained that there were people at the bar where Shepard, McKinney, and Henderson had first encountered each other who knew the perpetrators; for McKinney and Henderson to be seen "talking to a gay man and leaving with a gay guy" was potentially humiliating. Here we can see that even a crime of brutality linked to identity and motivated by strong feelings in the attackers is not equivalent to "hate." Rather, this crime was based on a need to exorcise the threat of humiliation that contact with Matthew Shepard might entail.

We could just say that Kristen Price was lying or was wrong in her understanding of the situation, but it is informative to take her at her word and think of what it might mean that hate was not the motive for this crime. What if McKinney and Henderson were more like the youths Franklin surveyed or the women Kathleen Blee interviewed? What if McKinney and Henderson were not hateful, but felt threatened? They felt threatened with loss of their privileged position in a (male) dominant public simply by being associated with someone in a minoritized position, in this case a gay man. This possibility gives us a different analytic purchase on a phenomenon—a "hate crime"—that so often seems to elude understanding. If hate crimes occur with such frightening regularity in a country where no one claims to hate anyone, then clearly an explanation other than "hate" is needed to account for such acts of extreme violence. The alternative we are proposing—that we use the frameworks of social division and justice, rather than hate and tolerance—also helps us to connect extreme forms of violence to more mundane social interactions and even to political debates. For example, the politicians who supported the Defense of Marriage Act (DOMA) in 1996 disclaimed homophobia. DOMA, which President Clinton signed into law, forbids federal recognition of same-sex marriage, and support for this law was framed in congressional debates as a matter of defending traditional American values. To its supporters, DOMA was not about discrimination against same-sex couples, it was about defense—of "the" American family. (Evidently, this American family does not or cannot recognize the gay men and lesbians in its midst.)

This is why the broad and rather abstract issue of who belongs to the "American public" has such important and practical implications, from who has the right to marry and who doesn't, to who can move safely through the streets of his or her own neighborhood and who cannot. Notions of who belongs and who does not are enforced in all sorts of ways, both apparently innocuous and lethally violent, and a focus on hate doesn't allow us to see connections between the everyday enforcement of these norms and deadly force. The mainstream values that mark some people and whole groups as "outsiders" can be the very same values that motivate and even justify violence; and again, this is not about hate.

Much of the press coverage of the police shooting of Amadou Diallo focused on the question of "hate." Diallo was fired upon forty-one times in the doorway of his Bronx apartment building by four police officers—despite the fact that he was unarmed and not involved in any violence. The police who shot him initially claimed that he looked like a rapist that they had been searching for; Diallo, however, bore little physical resemblance to the description of the suspect. News shows and talk shows posed the question over and over: "Were the officers driven to fire forty-one times by 'racial animus'?" We think this question is misplaced. Even if the officers did not personally hold racial animus, even if they were racially tolerant, they still may have been driven by the discriminatory set of assumptions that structure American public life. Since the time of the shooting there has been a review of the aggressive tactics and implicit racial profiling used by the New York Police Department's "street crime unit" of which these officers were a part, and many of these practices have been changed.[12] These officers operated in a racist atmosphere where they would stop and frisk persons on the street; in other words, they would treat them as criminal suspects based on their racial profile rather than on their behavior. It was this racist atmosphere, rather than any particular "animus" on the part of the officers, that made it all too likely that a tragedy like this shooting would occur. Diallo was treated as a threatening suspect, even though he had done nothing wrong.

A few weeks before New York City police fired forty-one shots at Amadou Diallo, four police officers in Riverside, California, fired nineteen times on Tyisha Miller as she sat in her car where she had passed out. According to the *New York Times,* Miller's cousin Anthonete Joiner and a friend called the police for help when they were unable to rouse Miller. Joiner reported that she told the police (three of whom were white and one Latino) that there was something wrong with Miller and that Miller had a gun on her lap. The police initially said that Miller had fired at the officers first, but later they admitted that they could find no evidence that Miller had fired the gun at all and changed their account to say that Miller had reached for the gun when one officer tried to wake her. According to her cousin, however, Tyisha Miller never woke up: "A couple of minutes later, they were shooting at her! She was just lying there the whole time."[13] Once again, we must ask, why did these officers fear an unconscious woman so much that they had to shoot her?

Unlike the police beating of Rodney King in 1991, the shootings of Miller and Diallo were not overtly racist events. There were no racial slurs shouted, no epithets used. The problem in both these cases was not hatred, but misperceptions about the level of threat that each of these people represented to the police. Neither Miller nor Diallo represented an actual threat to the lives of the police, and they certainly did not represent a threat equal to the level of force that was used against them. Nevertheless, in both cases the police felt threatened and used extreme force to quell that threat. The police believed that these shootings were about defense—their own. Why did these officers fear for their lives? What was so threatening about the unconscious Miller and the unarmed Diallo?

If we take seriously the officers' claim that they were acting out of self-defense, it means that Miller and Diallo weren't killed because the police believe that African Americans or Africans or people of color in general are so horrible they must die, but because they are seen as particularly threatening types of people. Egregious acts of violence are thus connected to the everyday violence of discrimination and oppression, to perceptions of who is and is not "one of us," who is and is not dangerous or a threat.

Instead of demonizing the particular police officers who killed Miller and Diallo or demonizing the police in general, we have to reckon with this disturbing possibility: the police were just acting on everyday perceptions. As such, the police shootings are not "exceptions to the rule" as much as they are extreme exemplifications of the rule itself. This analysis suggests that the structures that produce excessive violence are woven into the fabric of American values and self-understanding.

Tolerance is unfortunately implicated in this context of everyday violence—a context that is supposedly punctuated by and disconnected from moments of hate. Tolerance disavows violence and those who commit heinous crimes, but along the way it offers no exit from the us-them logic that structures hate and tolerance in our society. It also gives us no logical exit from the mandate to tolerate those who hate.

A correlative problem is that those who are placed in the category of "minority" have few options for responding publicly to their marginalization. They can

Figure 2. Cover image of *Newsweek* (June 21, 1993).

appeal to the paternalistic protection of those who represent the general public and the state. But this paternalism does not transform the us-them relation. (Think again of "The War Over Gays" and what's in a preposition.)

This us-them dynamic also establishes the "general public" as that with which "minorities" should identify and toward which they should aspire. Another term for this is "assimilation," a highly valorized concept in the story of "America, the melting pot." Only by acceding to the expectations of the "general public" can minorities expect any protections (such as they are) from the state. (And we have just seen something of the ambivalence of this protection in the cases of Miller, Diallo, and Michael Hardwick.)

What does it mean for those who have been minoritized that they must either identify with the "general public" (by whom they are only tolerated) or risk various forms of violence if they persist in their difference? The choices are rather stark: (1) assimilation to dominant norms, which may or may not provide protection and which certainly does not offer the freedom to be different; or (2) activism to change the structure of the general public— an activism that puts one at risk of being labeled an "extremist." What's so scary about difference? And what's so scary about activism? Isn't it part of democracy?

America is supposed to be a country that is open to all and in which everyone can participate in politics, but it is also the country in which the majority rules. It is no surprise, therefore, that there has been an ongoing tension between a majority that rules and various minorities whose rights have been (variously) denied and questioned. Thus there are two contrasting visions of the American public: one that includes everyone in America and another that encompasses only the majority. Various "others" are excluded from—if tolerated by—the second, more narrow, definition of the public.

This exclusionary public is seen in two early 1990s cover stories, both on the topic of lesbian and gay life. *Newsweek*'s June 21, 1993 cover jumps from "LESBIANS Coming Out Strong" to the anxious question, "What Are the Limits of Tolerance?" (Figure 2) Inside the cover, in the table of contents, *Newsweek* informs readers that, "On sitcoms and in Senate hearing rooms, Americans are finally getting a glimpse behind the old stereotypes and seeing the diversity of lesbian culture." Repeating the worry of its cover, *Newsweek* wonders, "But what are the limits of tolerance? Will the new visibility trigger a backlash?" (3) These questions frame lesbians and lesbianism as a problem that a larger American public has to negotiate and figure out. Although *Newsweek* goes on, in the accompanying article, to offer what it calls "stereotype-defying scene[s]" of lesbian life (54), up to and including lesbian couples with children, this larger "family" called America does not really include lesbians. If *Newsweek*'s assumed public did include lesbians, then lesbians would be more than worrisome objects of curiosity and tolerance. (Certainly, if lesbians were part of the America imagined and called up by *Newsweek*'s rhetorical frame, *Newsweek* could not then make the ridiculous claim that "Americans are finally getting a glimpse" of this previously invisible group. Presumably, some Americans, lesbian Americans, for example, had seen a lesbian before.)

Just two weeks after *Newsweek* worried over lesbians, another weekly newsmagazine jumped into the fray. The July 5, 1993 issue of *U.S. News and World Report* promised both "Straight Talk About Gays" and an "Exclusive Poll: Where A Concerned America Draws The Line" (Figure 3). Clearly, gay men and lesbians are not part of this "concerned" and generalized America; instead, they are the *objects* of concern, objects who may (or may not?) merit tolerance.

Being the object of tolerance does not represent full inclusion in American life, but rather a form of acceptance in which the boundary between us and them remains clear. We see this us-them boundary drawn and redrawn in so many different contexts. To take another example, part of the shock of the Columbine High School shootings in Littleton, Colorado, seemed to be that the shootings had occurred in a site—the suburbs, now the residence of 60 percent of the U.S. population—that is often identified with the general public, at least in its majoritarian form. As one letter to the editor in the *New York Times* bluntly put it: "Past homicide statistics were inflated by turf battles among gangs, which is violence in the service of a particular social subculture," while the Littleton shootings were an attack on "the social order as a whole."[14] Here, because neither the shooters nor the majority of the victims were members of identifiable "minority groups," because Eric Harris and Dylan Klebold were members of a "clique" (as the *Times* so often put it) and not a gang, because they shot at members of the dominant culture rather than members of a rival gang or subculture, the meaning of the shoot-

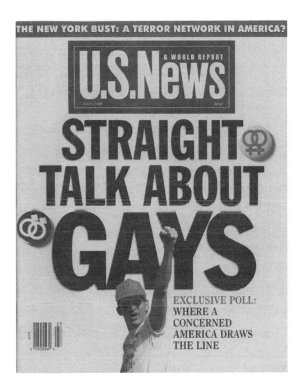

Figure 3. Cover image of *U.S. News and World Report* (July 5, 1993).

ings was different.[15] These shootings were a cause for national concern in a way that other school shootings were not.

Unlike the *Times*'s letter writer, we do not take for granted the categories "sub-cultural" and "the social," or, to underscore the issue, "minority" and "majority." The category of "minorities" appears to be self-evident, but is actually politically constructed. We certainly saw this in the case of Dr. Slepian when the *New York*

Times constructed women's right to abortion as a factional or minority issue, when in fact it is a constitutionally protected right in the United States.

This process of creating minorities does not just apply to women's issues or gay and lesbian issues. Earlier in this chapter, we pointed out how categories of religious and racial difference interacted in the early formation of U.S. national identity. This interaction has been part of the social construction of racial and ethnic categories, including the category "white." The history of whiteness has recently drawn a lot of attention from historians. Scholars of U.S. history have shown, for example, that who counts as "white" in America changed over the nineteenth and twentieth centuries, as the category "white" came to include many immigrant groups that were not initially considered "white." The title of Noel Ignatiev's history, *How the Irish Became White,* succinctly sums up this process, and similar stories can be told about Italians, Jews, and, in some cases, Germans.[16] These shifts in racial categorization have allowed white Americans to maintain a sense that people of color are always in the minority; as members of a minority group, people of color might be recipients of tolerance but can never be part of the tolerant majority. When minorities can't be so produced, there are problems for political discourse, as demonstrated by the frequently expressed public anxieties about what will happen over the next few decades when "caucasians" may no longer be in the statistical majority.

Yet even these anxieties hide the basic facts of our social relations. The very language about diversity—for example, references to "women and minorities"—erases the complexities of groups, hiding the fact that women are also members of various racial groups. When we consider "women and minorities" together we see that the only people not named by this combined category—white men—are certainly in the minority. The danger of recognizing what should be so glaringly obvious—namely, that those in our society with the most power, straight white Christian men, are in the minority—is that then we could no longer simply discount power imbalances as the necessary inequalities of a country in which "majority rules." Nor could we pass off "hate crimes" as isolated incidents enacted by a few extremists who have not learned the lesson of tolerance.

Because we're so confused about the majority-minority relation in the United States, we're unable to see how certain forms of violence are not just expressions of hatred and extremism, but rather are part of our everyday world. Let us attend for a moment to the ways in which violence against women—unfortunately an everyday occurrence in U.S. society—does and does not feature in political debates about "hate crimes." The 1990 Federal Hate Crimes Statistics Act, signed into law by President George H. W. Bush, directs the Justice Department to collect annual data on crimes motivated by the victim's race, religion, ethnicity, or sexual orientation. Sex or gender is not among the categories of analysis for this law. In practice, this means that the law in no way directs the Justice Department to collect data on crimes against women as women.

The omission of gender from that Act was not accidental. The National Organization for Women had lobbied strenuously—but ultimately unsuccessfully—for its inclusion. Why was gender left out of the 1990 Federal Hate Crimes Statistics Act? A variety of reasons was supplied at the time. Some opponents of collecting data on hate crimes against women argued that it would only duplicate other documentation on crimes against women. The Justice Department already keeps statistics on the number of male-female rapes reported annually, as do most state and local jurisdictions. However, when male-female rapes are reported and counted, they are not analyzed and interpreted for the possibility that gender bias may have animated the attack. If gender bias does get admitted as a motive, it is either particularized as hatred against this woman and this woman only, or particularized in another way as this particular man's hatred against women in general. In either instance, gender bias is framed as a problem of individual deviance rather than a general cultural phenomenon.

This inability or refusal to reckon with the general problem of violence against women has hardly gone away. One decade after the first President Bush signed the

Federal Hate Crimes Statistics Act, there is still much congressional opposition to including gender in the new Federal Hate Crimes Prevention Act. To call crimes based on gender "hate crimes" would imply that every time a woman was raped and every time a woman was beaten was a "hate crime." To do so would undercut the entire structure of cordoning off and containing those who hate and those who are hated from the "general public." Both the perpetrators and the victims of violence against women are too generalized to allow for recognition of this violence as tied to the hatred that Americans so often attribute only to extremists.

Our proposed solution to this dilemma would not be simply to add gender-based violence to the category of "hate crimes." There may be good practical reasons to do so, such as increased funding for domestic violence shelters. Conceptually, however, "hate crimes" as a category perpetuates an understanding of American public life as divided between a clear majority and distinct minorities. The possibility that gender bias could motivate violence against women is so confounding because "hate crimes" are assumed to be perpetrated by an intolerant and extremist "minority" against members of "minority" groups, and yet women are not, statistically speaking, a minority.

As we've suggested above, the category of tolerance, which is supposed to combat "hate crimes," depends upon these very same "minoritizing" assumptions. If we could recognize the complicated relations between gender and sexuality and among gender, sexuality, race, class, and physical ability, we would recognize that the majority of Americans are in some way the potential, if not already actual, objects of discrimination. This recognition would change our basic approach to hatred and to the discrimination on which hatred is based. We would need to look not toward tolerating "minorities," but toward reconstructing our public life so that everyone is included in categories like "the general public," "the public at large," or "all Americans."

At one level this claim to inclusion is a basic liberal claim, but it will remain a radical demand as long as dominant American conceptions of "the public" can so easily slip into "majority rules." In the end there are two sets of American public values—the values of freedom and justice for all, and the values in which the general public dominates minorities. These two distinct ways of looking at the world are akin to the distinction between religious tolerance and religious freedom. We advocate the value of freedom rather than tolerance, because freedom opens up the possibility that an expansive, rather than a narrowly majoritarian, public might be built in America.

3   Not Born That Way

In his blistering dissent in *Romer v. Evans* (which we discussed at length in chapter 1) Supreme Court Justice Antonin Scalia accused homosexuals (and their advocates) of dedicating themselves "to achieving not merely a grudging social toleration, but full social acceptance, of homosexuality." Our view of the matter is rather different: we think homosexuals (and their advocates) have been asking for far too little. Lesbian and gay advocates have been asking for tolerance and equal rights, not freedom and equal justice. They have accommodated their political arguments and legal strategies to the us-them structure of tolerance (which we criticized in chapter 2). They haven't challenged the exclusionary nature of the "general public" in which difference from dominant norms must be minimized as a condition of belonging or membership.

In practice this has meant bringing together two apparently competing arguments about gay identity: an assimilationist, or universalizing, argument that minimizes any difference from the "general public" and a minoritizing approach that allows for lesbian and gay difference but analogizes this difference to the constitutionally protected categories of sex, and especially race.[1] Both of these tacks—assimilationist and minoritizing—focus on identity and bracket questions of conduct or practice. But as we have seen in chapter 1, first, the identity-act relation is an unstable one, and second, the issue of "homosexual conduct" cannot be so easily sidestepped. Certainly, the issue of homosexual conduct cannot be sidestepped if we are interested in the freedom not simply to be gay, but the freedom to "do" gay. In this chapter we'll explore why lesbian and gay advocates so often frame their arguments in such narrow terms. As we will show, the dominant ways of arguing for "gay rights" do not simply offer limited and limiting models for sexual freedom, but they also pose real risks for social justice, including racial justice.

Opponents of lesbian and gay rights have overwhelmingly depicted homosexuality as a behavior-based identity, as a lifestyle choice only, and a bad choice at that. Proponents of lesbian and gay rights have responded by portraying homosexual identity as innate, in some way rooted in an individual's essential nature. Here, for instance, is journalist and openly gay neoconservative commentator Andrew Sullivan responding to Reverend Jerry Falwell's and Reverend Albert Mohler Jr.'s (President of the Southern Baptist Theological Seminary) characterization of homosexuality as a willfully chosen behavior: "Homosexuality is not a behavior. It is something we are. It is a deep and integral part of our personality. It is a deep and integral part of our soul." (Sullivan made these comments during a televised debate on "Larry King Live," on October 17, 1998, the evening after Matthew Shepard's funeral.)

As literary scholar Eve Kosofsky Sedgwick points out, the claim that homosexuality is immutable—unchangeable—is frequently motivated by a desire to "insulat[e]" gay and lesbian identity from "societal interference," moral condemnation, and even eradication.[2] The "born that way" argument is not simply a matter of political strategy or convenience; it is also a sincerely held view.

Many gay men, lesbians, bisexuals, and transgender people would describe their identities as inborn, something they were aware of from a very young age. At a minimum, they would say that they could not be other than who and what they are.

It may even be that the claim, "I was born this way," is a way of describing this feeling of unchosenness, this sense that the "I" could not be any other way. However, once this way of narrating and making sense of an individual's identity gets put into play as a political strategy for an entire group, the political and moral implications of such assertions must be scrutinized. While we understand both the political and experiential stakes of grounding gay and lesbian identities in an individual's essential nature, we also believe the "born that way" approach has serious, even dangerous, limitations.

The "born that way" argument is poised against both secular and Christian-inflected, biblically based arguments against lesbian and gay rights, but it works better against secular-scientistic homophobia. This is because biblically based homophobia can have it both ways. It can object to homosexuality on the grounds that homosexuality contravenes divine purpose and it can object to homosexuality on the grounds that it is contra nature. On this view, divine purpose may or may not correspond to nature's laws.

A fascinating and revealing example of this rhetorical shuttling between scientistic appeals to nature and religious appeals to God's law is found in Alveda King's testimony, in May 1999, before a joint House-Senate Judiciary Committee of the Massachusetts legislature. King, the niece of Martin Luther King, Jr., was testifying in favor of a Massachusetts version of the Defense of Marriage Act (DOMA); her visit to Boston was arranged by conservative groups backing the antigay bill. In her testimony, King cited scripture to make her case for DOMA and against same-sex marriage. The biblical passages she selected were, in her view, unambiguous condemnations of homosexuality and by implication of same-sex marriage. A member of the joint committee pressed King on her use of the Bible and asked her to respond to the striking coincidence that opponents of civil rights for African Americans in the fifties and sixties had also drawn upon the Bible—and indeed on some of the very same passages King was citing—to justify their racism as divinely sanctioned. In reply, King shifted the ground of her objection to homosexuality and same-sex marriage from theology to biology. She told lawmakers that they should not "confuse skin color with sexual orientation."[3] The comparison between homosexuality and race was invalid; African Americans, she argued, were denied civil rights because of an immutable characteristic, something in their very nature, which they could not change. But homosexuality, according to King, is a behavior-based identity, something homosexuals have chosen; it is not natural and, thus, not deserving of protection.

There are good reasons to resist an analogy between sexual orientation and race, but they are not the reasons King supplies. In fact, we need to look at the logical entailment of King's argument: the only reason race is a constitutionally protected category is because people of color cannot change; they were born that way. What does this imply for racial justice? We'll come back to this question.

In a context framed by the type of biblical or "Christianized" homophobia that King promotes, proponents of lesbian and gay rights have sometimes tried to out-exegete their opponents. Let's return to the October 17, 1998, broadcast of "Larry King Live." If Matthew Shepard's murder provided the immediate context for the televised debate, the telecast also provided an opportunity—ultimately a wasted one—to discuss the terms under which homosexuality and gay rights could properly be addressed and argued over in public life. A particular flash point was a series of full-page national advertisements, taken out by fifteen conservative organizations in the summer of 1998, promoting the idea that homosexuality is chosen behavior, not immutable identity. To rebut this view, Elizabeth Birch, director of the Human Rights Campaign, the largest and best funded national organization for lesbian and gay rights, tried her hand at biblical exegesis. In response to the question directed at her by guest host Wolf Blizter ("What do you say to the argument that Reverend Jerry Falwell is a theologian and he is strictly going by what the Bible says about homosexuality?") Birch argued:

> Everyone is a sinner. Reverend Falwell is a sinner. He had a very unruly teenagehood. The fact is that those messages [the newspaper advertisements] miss the central message of the scripture, and the central message of the scripture is about love, and it's about unity and not about division and divisive messages.

Note what Birch does *not* say. She does *not* mention the separation of church and state; she does *not* remind the audience that in the United States, no single religion—in fact, no religion at all—is established as the one and true religion. At no point in her response does she suggest that even if the Reverend Falwell's interpretation of scripture were correct, his theological perspective should not and cannot dictate the application of state and federal laws. Instead, she casts her argument in Falwell's terms (in the language of Christian values and biblical truths) and seeks to displace his homophobic interpretation with a gay-affirmative one. This theological turn does not challenge the Christianized terms of discussion; it accedes to them.

In fairness to Birch, in the particular public space she was then occupying, "Larry King Live," and in view of the representatives of the "other" side (two men whose authority derives from their ministries, Reverend Jerry Falwell and Reverend Albert Mohler, Jr.), her theological gambit may be seen as a canny attempt to co-opt their terms. It may also have seemed to Birch to be the only rhetorical path available to her, given the way the debate was being framed.

Has lesbian and gay politics come down to this? To counter antigay laws, pronouncements, and even violence, advocates for gay rights must play not just the biology game (for example, "born that way"), but also the Bible game, arguing about what the Bible really does or does not say about homosexuality? This form of argumentation does not make more room for difference. In fact, it reinforces a Christian public sphere.

In July 1998 a coalition of fifteen conservative Christian and ex-gay groups took out full-page ads in the *New York Times, USA Today,* and the *Washington Post,* among other papers, promising "hope and healing for homosexuals." The names of the sponsoring organizations appeared at the bottom of the advertisement, their names introduced in this way: "*In the public interest, this message was paid for by the following organizations, representing millions of American families*" (italics in original). The sponsoring organizations were Alliance for Traditional Marriage-Hawaii, American Family Association, Americans for Truth about Homosexuality, Center for Reclaiming America, Christian Family Network, Christian Coalition, Citizens for Community Values, Colorado for Family Values, Concerned Women for America, Coral Ridge Ministries, Family First, Family Research Council, Liberty Counsel, National League Foundation, and Kerusso Ministries.[4] This last group, Kerusso Ministries, is an "ex-gay" organization; it even sponsors an annual "National Coming Out of Homosexuality Day" (which takes place, appropriately, the day after "National Coming Out Day"). Donald Wildmon, the high-profile head of the American Family Association, has praised "National Coming Out of Homosexuality Day" as "a means whereby to dispel the lies of the homosexual rights crowd who say they are born that way and cannot change."[5]

The sophisticated ad campaign of July 1998 took aim at these same "lies." The first ad, which appeared in the *New York Times* on July 13, received the most media attention; it featured Anne Paulk, "wife, mother, former lesbian" (Figure

Figure 4. Full-page advertisement in *New York Times* (July 13, 1998), A11.

4).[6] The ad's text unfolds as a first-person narrative; quotation marks set off each new section of text to authenticate the narrative as Anne Paulk's own. "I'm living proof," the ad begins, "that Truth can set you free." Before presenting an account of Paulk's coming to lesbianism and her coming out of it, the text offers this anticipatory justification for the outrage the ad is calculated to produce:

"Recently, several prominent people like Trent Lott, Reggie White, and Angie and Debbie Winans have spoken out on homosexuality . . . calling it a sin. When I was living as a lesbian I didn't like hearing words like that . . . until I realized that God's love was truly meant for me." (italics, quotation marks, and ellipses in original)

The ad is a carefully structured interplay of text and image. A close-up of Paulk fills the upper third of the full-page ad, and a diamond ring and wedding band adorn her hand, signaling her newfound relationships to God, husband, and self.

Interestingly, the relationship enabled by her coming out of homosexuality is not a relation to a man, but to God and Truth. Indeed, in an italicized aside, which occupies the center of the full-page ad, another narrative voice—that of the sponsoring organizations—interrupts as if to comment on Paulk's individual story and the promise it holds out to all homosexuals: *"Thousands of ex-gays like these have walked away from their homosexual identities. While the paths each took into homosexuality may vary, their stories of hope and healing through the transforming love of Jesus Christ are the same."* In the place of love of the same, there is the same love for all: Jesus Christ's. Ultimately, the ad does not narrate a transition to a new *sexual* identity, but to a newly found *sectarian* one.

This is not to say that the ad presents the choice between homosexuality and heterosexuality as a matter of moral indifference. Far from it: the conversion narrative clearly presents Paulk's former lesbian identity as a profound misstep, one launched by the immoral actions of others, but exacerbated by Paulk's own bad choices. We want to make clear at this juncture that just as we value the way that individual gay men and lesbians tell the story of their identity, so too are we willing to grant Paulk her story, her way of telling her own identity. However, we can allow for the sincerity of Paulk's ex-gay conversion narrative even as we also critically assess the way her individual story is being framed for a public audience and put to decidedly political use. Why, we must ask, is Paulk's sectarian conversion presented as being "in the public interest"?

The story of Paulk's undoing and ultimate redemption unfolds over the course of seven sections of text; each narrative unit is set off by a boldface section heading that encapsulates the section's main theme. The first section is entitled "One boy's sin and the making of a lesbian," and in it we discover the traumatic core of Paulk's lesbianism: "I was four years old when a teenage boy molested me. When he warned me not to say anything, I went silent. But as I grew, the pain wouldn't stay quiet."[7] The next section ("Being a woman became a mystery") continues the causal narrative, linking the sexual violation Paulk experienced as a girl to her growing discomfort with being a woman:

> "By the time I hit my teens I was rough . . . my heart cold. I believed being "feminine" meant being weak and vulnerable . . . so looking and dressing hard felt right. I had so thoroughly rejected my own femininity that, even though I had a lot of male friends, I just wasn't attracted to men sexually. I became drawn to other women who had what I felt was missing in me. But the pain inside kept yelling." (italics, ellipses, and quotation marks in original)

The sexual injury experienced by Paulk as a young girl has resulted in two related traumas: an inability to identify properly with her "own" sex and a corresponding inability to desire the "opposite" sex. Paulk's later same-sex object-choice comes across as a deferred response to molestation; her lesbianism is acquired, not innate. What's more, because her same-sex desires are depicted as emerging out of sexual violation, her lesbian identity is a *coerced* acquisition, not something she would have chosen for herself.[8]

This theme of sexual exploitation returns in the third section of the text, but with an interesting twist. Section three ("There's a God-shaped hole in everyone's heart") finds Paulk at college, where she comes out as a lesbian and into the gay college scene. Paulk's coming out story implicates a gay college counselor and the campus gay and lesbian group as coauthors of her lesbianism. The narrative effectively plots her homosexual experiences in college as a continuation of the earlier scene of childhood (heterosexual) molestation. The insinuation is that lesbianism is not just caused by molestation; it is itself a form of molestation. The teenage boy was Paulk's first molester; the "gay college counselor who affirmed [Paulk's] feelings [for women]" was another.

Paulk's coming out story is not a happy one; she is fighting herself—fighting for herself—at every step. We follow her turn to prayer as she seeks a way out of the lesbian life. As befits the conventions of the conversion narrative, Paulk's spiritual struggle is not a straight path, but a circuitous and surprising route home, to what the narrative calls the "real healing" of God's love.

In staging Paulk's self-discovery as a coming out of lesbianism narrative, the ad brilliantly recasts the relations between homosexuality and heterosexuality, narrative and truth. It is heterosexuality, not homosexuality, that gets poised as the underdog; heterosexual *and* Christian identity is the truth that a too-permissive culture would relativize away.[9]

Lesbian and gay rights' groups' response to this campaign was to take out gay-affirmative full-page ads in the same papers in which the initial antigay advertisements had appeared. One such ad appeared in the *New York Times,* on July 19, 1998, and was explicitly framed with and against Anne Paulk's ex-gay narrative (Figure 5). Like the antigay ad, this progay response mixes image and text, and its organizing narrative is similarly subdivided into seven individually named sections. The ad was sponsored by a coalition of groups and individuals: Gay and Lesbian Alliance Against Defamation, Gay and Lesbian Victory Fund Foundation, Gay, Lesbian and Straight Education Network, The Gill Foundation, Andrew Tobias and Charles Nolan, Human Rights Campaign Foundation, An Uncommon Legacy Foundation, National Black Lesbian and Gay Leadership

Figure 5. Full-page advertisement in *New York Times* (July 19, 1999), 17.

Forum, National Center for Lesbian Rights, National Gay and Lesbian Task Force, National Latina/o LGBT Organization, National Youth Advocacy Coalition, and Parents, Families and Friends of Lesbians and Gays. The Human Rights Campaign Foundation produced the ad. Like the fifteen groups who sponsored the antigay ads, the thirteen progay groups also claimed the public interest—and with the same billing notice: *"In the public interest, this message was paid for by the following organizations, representing millions of American families"* (italics in original).

Where the antigay ad gestured "toward hope and healing for homosexuals," the progay ad addressed itself "toward hope and healing for America." The face of America is supplied by Dave, Ruth, and Margie Waterbury, the smiling white family gazing out from the upper third of the full-page ad. If Anne Paulk is "living proof that Truth can set you free," the Waterburys—father, mother, and daughter—are "living proof that families with lesbian and gay kids can be whole, happy and worthy of all that this great country promises."

The first-person narrator of this ad is plural, not an "I" but a "we"—significantly, the "we" of Margie's parents. Margie's voice is absent from the narrative; the lesbian daughter is spoken about and for, but does not speak for herself. This is a telling decision, one that reveals much about the complex of assumptions undergirding the ad. Given that the antigay ad was constructed in the voice of an individual ex-lesbian protagonist, we might have expected the progay ad to counter with the personal story of a self-identified "practicing" lesbian. But this ad is cultivating the "middle," attempting to speak not just to "the heart of America" but *from* it. The ad's boldface reminder, "Minnesota is in the heart of America," does more than specify the Waterburys' geographic home. It identifies them as occupants of the symbolic center, the American middle ground. Of course, many gay men and lesbians live in the middle west; presumably the Waterburys' daughter Margie is among them. But lesbians and gay men do not and, arguably, cannot occupy the symbolic "heart" of America. The very terms of the debate have already rendered them "extremists." This lesbian daughter—no matter how "mainstream" her views, no matter her zip code—cannot speak on behalf of those values of reason and tolerance that distinguish the center from its margins.

In the previous chapter, we examined how the emergence and legitimacy of "the middle" and its fantasized "tolerance" depend on the construction of two opposed sides. Not only are these two sides opposed to each other, but more importantly, they are also opposed to precisely the values of reason, tolerance, and civility the middle comes to represent. This analysis helps us to understand how the progay ad works, but it is not an understanding that provides any comfort. The progay ad does not simply speak to the middle; it actively participates in its ongoing construction.

If the center embodies the values of reason, tolerance, and civility just named, this embodiment is made manifest through faith and family. Faith and family are not neutral values, however, but themselves encode particular norms of Christianity and heterosexuality. It is no accident that the family selected to represent American values is white, from the middle west, active members of a Christian denomination, reproductive (they have two daughters; the other daughter "happens to be heterosexual," the Waterburys tell us in the first section of the text), and Republican. In the next-to-last section of the narrative ("Equal rights, not special rights") the Waterburys assure us that their plea for tolerance and equality is nonideological because they "happen to be Republicans." In a political context where gay rights have been "assigned" to the Democratic party, the Waterburys' Republican credentials function, paradoxically, to assure us of their impartiality and moderation.

Significantly, the progay ad does not attempt to counter the "homosexuals can change" argument through an appeal to origins. Indeed, the ad entirely skirts the question of what "causes" homosexuality.[10] This would be a major accomplishment if the ad did not exchange one governing opposition (Is homosexuality acquired or innate?) for another (Are homosexuals just like us, or not?). That the ad answers in the affirmative—homosexuals are just like us!—is no great advance when the "we" enacted and assumed by the ad already leaves so many outside its bounds.

The gay-affirmative ad is a point for point rejoinder to the ex-gay narrative of Anne Paulk. It seeks to legitimate gay identity by taking up and reusing the terms of the ex- (and anti-) gay ad. As an initial political response, the gay-affirmative ad was absolutely necessary. Its short-term effectiveness, however, does not mitigate its high longer-term costs. The progay ad reasserts a conservative approach to both homosexuality and religion. It does not contest or reverse the terms of the antigay ad, but rather recycles them. Within the terms of the ad, the tolerance claimed for homosexuality is a specifically Christian tolerance. The values staked out for and by the ad are Christian values, as if the language of values can only be run through a discourse of religion. The gay-affirming ad does not challenge the cultural centrality of Reform Protestantism, then, but even re-asserts it in the name of tolerance.

The discrepancy between short-term, "local" tactics and goals and their longer-term effects is noteworthy. The progay ad speaks the language of "the center." Yet we need to consider how this phantom center functions to solicit identifications with an idealized "we the people" as well as the fact that this "we" does not speak for all. Unfortunately, by framing the debate in the language of Christian values, both the antigay ad and the gay-affirming one present very limited ways of thinking about and enacting connections among sexual practices, identities, and values. Despite their apparently opposed viewpoints, both ads promote a narrow vision of the good life. If for the antigay ad being a good Christian means being heterosexual, for the progay ad being a good homosexual means being Christian. Are our options really that narrow?

The point-counterpoint approach of the gay-affirmative ad labors under a misconception of how homophobia works. It is not the truth or falsity of particular claims about who homosexuals really "are" that needs to be challenged, but rather how such claims are deployed, how they legitimate some subjects and delegitimate others, if they recognize them at all. In light of this, we urge a shift in focus away from the content of particular propositions about homosexuality to the *way* these propositions circulate and operate culturally.[11] In practice, this redirection is a caution against trying to out-reason and out-exegete homophobia, as if falsifying homophobic pronouncements were sufficient to assure equal rights, civility, or even grudging "tolerance."

This qualification seems especially urgent in the case of biblically based pronouncements against homosexuality. The temptation to play "the Bible game" will be strong. But turning to what the Bible "really" says about homosexuality reasserts the cultural authority of the Bible and the political pronouncements of its interpreters. (We think we are on safe ground when we predict that some traditions of biblical interpretation will be given wider public credence than others.) Now, there may well be local contexts in which it makes sense to engage in biblical interpretation and argument. For example, individuals active in their synagogue or church may want to engage biblical passages as a matter of religious practice and not simply as political strategy. What we are objecting to is allowing "the" Bible to frame public discussions of sexuality. But this is what Elizabeth Birch does.

Moreover, as we have already tried to suggest, there is no such thing as winning the "truth of homosexuality" game. Homophobia does not rise and fall on the coherence of its claims. Quite the contrary. As David M. Halperin argues in *Saint Foucault,* you falsify one claim—and taken individually, they are usually easy claims to disqualify—and another will take its place, sometimes even a claim directly contrary to the hydra's head you have just lopped off. But the incoherence and contradictions of homophobic discourse do not incapacitate it; rather, they keep this particular monster alive. You say that homosexuals are not sinners, lapsed moral agents, who have willfully chosen to act contrary to God's law or the law of nature? Fine, then we will take homosexuality out of the churches and out of the courts and transfer it to medical experts, who might assess the anterior region of a particular hypothalamic region or tweak the am-niotic fluid of the developing protohomosexual fetus.

When it comes to homosexuality, heterosexuality speaks out of both sides of its mouth, but without its message being disqualified on those grounds. Think back to Trent Lott's toggle between describing homosexuality as a sin and analo-gizing it to physical addiction (alcoholism) and psychological "disturbances" (sex addiction and kleptomania). Or recall the legislative testimony of Alveda King, whose opposition to homosexuality and gay rights moved easily between a discourse of Christian morality and a discourse of nature. Christianized ho-mophobia does not have to decide between opposing homosexuality as contra nature or opposing it as contra divine purpose.

Here is another example of contradiction at work in the service of homo-phobia. A familiar staple of antigay discourse is the claim that exposure to the mere fact of homosexuality's existence can overthrow a person's "natural" het-erosexual identity. What is fascinating about this line of argument is the implied vulnerability of heterosexuality. On the one hand, everyone is really heterosex-ual. On the other, exposure to homosexual possibilities at too young an age (and the age that is too young seems to have neither basement nor ceiling) can per-vert nature's course.

An interesting version of this fantasy appears in Jerry Falwell's much-mocked 1998 "outing" of the children's television character "Tinky Winky." Falwell's warning to parents—that Tinky Winky's homosexuality might entice their children into the homosexual "lifestyle"—depends on a particular Chris-tian theological conception of human nature. In this worldview, human na-ture is vulnerable to the distorting effects of culture. Falwell's worry that Tinky Winky is coming for your heterosexual child is an apocalyptic vision of cul-tural determinism, in which an immoral culture overrides ever-corruptible human nature. This is why opposition to the so-called homosexual agenda often clusters around children, who serve as placeholders for larger cultural anxieties about changes in national identity, gender relations, and family structure. Because homosexuals cannot reproduce, this strain of thought goes, they must recruit. In their innocence and openness to new things, children—the nation's future and the family's guarantee—are held to be especially vulnerable to homosexual missionizing. One too many episode of "Teletubbies," or "Ellen," and there goes the nation.

Attempts to advance the morality of a queer way of life need to move beyond refutations of Christian-inflected claims about homosexuality or sexuality in general in which we (whoever "we" are) counter their "homosexuals are like that" and "sex is for this" with our "are not like that; do too want this." We need to develop other ways of thinking and doing sexual subjectivity, ways that do not demand the Faustian bargain of saying once for all who and what we are. Instead of ceding the question of sexual values to opponents of lesbian and gay rights, as the born that way approach does; and instead of reinforcing the cultural authority of the Bible, as seeking to out-interpret explicitly biblical homophobia does, we want to develop an alternative paradigm for sexual identity *and* sexual justice. We also need to develop a richer language of sexual values and ethics, one that does not require coming out for or against the Bible. Can sexual values only speak through the language of Christianity?

Both the progay and the antigay ads are caught up in an ongoing impasse over the "origins" of homosexuality. What causes it? Where do homosexuals come from, and won't they please go away? To do an end run around this impasse has seemed impossible for many gay rights activists in part because of the force with which the antigay conversion narrative is promulgated, but also because of a historical tendency to frame lesbian and gay rights claims through a paradigm of "race" and by analogy to the civil rights claims of African Americans. Just as we are concerned with the overall implications of the "born that way" argument, this correlative "homosexuality is like race" argument has serious limitations, not the least of which is the way this analogy flattens important historical differences between the way racism and homophobia work.

The "like race" argument depends on naturalized notions of race, as well as essentialized and naturalized notions of sexuality. By anchoring gay rights claims in a civil rights paradigm dependent on "benign immutable difference" (born that way), advocates for lesbian and gay rights participate in the mystification of race, sex, and now sexuality. They forget that historically the naturalization of racial and sexual difference has more often been used to justify discrimination than to prevent it. (Besides, making sex and race discrimination illegal, as the 1964 Civil Rights Act did, has hardly ended it.)

Even more importantly, "born that way" arguments were not an absolutely required component of antidiscrimination law. As legal scholars Janet E. Halley and David A. J. Richards have both argued, physical immutability has not been the only criterion used by the courts to justify equal protection doctrine.[12] In fact, as Halley points out, immutability has played a relatively minor role until recently (50, 66).

Halley goes on to show that gay rights advocates have focused on the moments when the courts, "in the course of justifying . . . equal protection doctrine, had observed that race and sex were 'immutable characteristics'" (50). In arguing for gay rights, advocates have crafted their own legal briefs so as to make immutability the leading edge of the argument rather than one component among others. And they specifically linked the putative immutability of homosexuality to the putative immutability of race. Like race, homosexuality is unchosen, and just as it is illegal to discriminate on the (unchosen) basis of race, so too should it be illegal to discriminate on the (unchosen) basis of sexual orientation. Or so the argument goes. But these legal strategies in which homosexuality is analogized to race so as to assert the immutability of homosexuality have failed miserably in the courts.

Although "homosexuality is like race" arguments have been unsuccessful in advancing gay rights through the courts, they have had unforeseen consequences on the other side of the analogy. Halley identifies a deeply disquieting effect of this analogical thinking. She suggests that the rhetoric of "special rights," which opponents of lesbian and gay rights have so brilliantly (and disingenuously) used to recast equal rights for lesbians and gays as fewer rights for everyone else, has been taken up by conservative opponents of affirmative action. Among the ironies of this rhetorical drift, in which the language of "special rights" comes to characterize and disqualify affirmative action for racial mi norities and women, is that the "gay rights is special rights" equation was sometimes tailored to appeal specifically to African Americans and other racial and ethnic minorities.[13] Yet, once lesbian and gay efforts to secure the same legal protections that the 1964 Civil Rights Act gave racial and ethnic minorities and women are recast as "special rights," it is no real stretch to characterize *all* antidiscrimination ordinances and laws as "special rights."

The rhetorical expansion of "special rights" to cover not just gay rights in particular but civil rights protections in general is not the only problematic effect of the "like race" analogy. Halley locates another, when she argues that during the 1990s courts have come, increasingly, to make immutability a prerequisite of suspect status classification. Gay "like race" appeals, with their stress on immutability, must, she says, bear some responsibility for this interpretive narrowing.

Even assuming, however, that race or sex were matters of immutable difference (an assumption we do not share), we wonder at any argument that would defend civil rights on the ground of nature. This kind of reasoning is limited, and on numerous counts. "Born that way" arguments can have the unanticipated effect of separating identity from practice. Such arguments may create a space for homosexual identity, but they can also allow for the regulation of what is often euphemistically called "homosexual conduct."

In other words, it might be okay to be homosexual, but it is not okay to act on homosexual desire. This is the world of "don't ask, don't tell," the current policy on "gays in the military." This policy was supposed to be a "compromise" that would allow gay and lesbian people to serve in the military without harassment or threat of discharge as long as they remained silent about their homosexuality. Instead, according to Pentagon statistics, the effects of the policy have been higher than ever rates of discharge and harassment.[14]

The analogy to race and sex that the "born that way" argument so often leans upon is also deeply troubling for its assumptions about the value of racial and sexual differences from the "norm." What, after all, are the implications of saying that civil rights depend upon innate physical or biological characteristics? Let's examine the implicit moral imperative to such a claim. Supposedly innate characteristics, race and sex, could only be an issue if there is an underlying assumption that there is something wrong or, at minimum, less desirable with being other than the dominant identity (white and/or male). If individuals could pick and choose their race or sex (and remember that many opponents of gay rights imagine that gay men and lesbians blithely pick and choose their sexual "preferences"), could they be required either to become the model American or to suffer discrimination? As extreme as this scenario sounds, it is, in fact, the ultimate logic of justifying civil rights protections on the ground of nature.

Where do such assertions land us? Characteristics that are taken to be immutable, such as skin color or sex, will be tolerated. But when traits or behaviors are taken to be discretionary and volitional, people can be asked, indeed compelled, to change their behavior and assimilate to dominant norms. This puts us right back in the realm of love the sinner, hate the sin. Gay identity may be protected by the courts (as it was in *Romer*), but "homosexual conduct" certainly is not (as we have seen in *Hardwick*).

However, as Halley noted and we want to underscore, this is not just a problem for sexuality. If we say that we should not discriminate against women, for example, because sex difference is innate, are we saying that it is only okay to be a woman because they—women—can't help it? In other words, there is a very big difference between claiming that we should not discriminate against women because sexual difference is innate, and claiming that we should not discriminate against women because it is okay or even good to be a woman.

Let's look at an example at the intersection of race and sex, *Rogers v. American Airlines, Inc.*[15] This 1981 case concerned Renee Rogers, an African American woman employed as an airport operations officer by American Airlines. American Airlines enforced a grooming policy for its employees that banned all braided hairstyles. Rogers, whose hair was fully braided, was given the "option" of changing her hairstyle or being fired. Instead she sued, asserting that the policy violated Title VII's protections against both race and sex discrimination.

As legal scholar Kenji Yoshino says in his recent analysis of this case, on its face the grooming policy was both race- and sex-neutral; it applied to blacks as well as whites, to women as well as men.[16] The courts certainly saw the policy this way. Yoshino relates that the federal court dismissed Rogers's claim of race discrimination on the grounds that, first, hairstyle is easily changed and second, even if hairstyle (in this instance, cornrows) were associated with a particular racial group, hair did not constitute an impermissible basis for discrimination. The court also dismissed Rogers's claim of sex discrimination, holding that the airline's grooming policy did not discriminate on the basis of any immutable characteristic (Yoshino 6). Yoshino believes the court's reasoning is flawed. What does it mean to say that race and sex are protected categories when traits and behaviors expressive of race and sex difference—including how one does one's hair—are not protected? Renee Rogers may have been protected from being fired for "being" black and for "being" a woman, but the court did not see fit to protect her from being fired for the way she expressed her identity as an African American woman. In effect, the grooming policy, with the federal court's ultimate endorsement, forced her to choose between adopting a hairstyle expressive of dominant racial and gender norms and forfeiting her job. This is no choice at all.

"Born that way" arguments, then, do not give us strong grounds for protecting conduct, whether that conduct be associated with gender, race, and/or sexuality. Additionally, there are good historical reasons for objecting to born that way arguments. As noted above, grounding racial and sexual difference in nature has more often worked in the service of discrimination, rather than against it. We should not forget that both slavery and racial segregation (in other words, some of the most painful experiences in the history of the United States) were defended on the grounds of nature. The idea that sex differences are natural has been no less pernicious for women.

Nor do we need to settle the question of what part (if any) of race, sex, and sexuality is biological. This is because biological difference is not itself the issue; the problem is the way that biology is mapped onto moral distinction, a mapping that ends up turning difference into a matter of superiority and inferiority. In our view, biological arguments should not be the basis for antidiscrimination ordinances. We need to develop persuasive accounts for the value, rather than mere toleration, of difference.

As we have noted earlier, there are sincere and sincerely contested beliefs about the origins of sexual identity, and this is not just a contest between opponents and proponents of gay rights. Gay men, lesbians, and bisexuals are themselves hardly in agreement as to the "origins" of their sexual desires and feelings. Some would say they experience their sexuality as innate; others understand their sexual orientation as a mixture of chosen and unchosen factors; and still others narrate their sexuality as volitional, perhaps reframing their sexual preferences as a question of political preferences. (If we turn our attention to the contested areas of racial and gender identity, there too we find that individuals have very different ways of describing their experiences and self-understandings.)

Nonetheless, the appeal to nature is attractive in the contemporary moment because it seems to avoid intractable moral arguments about homosexuality and religion. Rather than directly engaging the charges that homosexuality is wrong, advocates for gay and lesbian rights have by and large attempted to evade the moral and religious questions altogether by retreating to the supposedly amoral or supramoral realm of nature. Unfortunately, as we have just argued, "the biological" is not separate from the "moral." Moreover, avoiding the moral basis for many people's objections to homosexuality ends up ceding all moral language and claims to opponents of homosexuality and gay rights. (Additionally, as we saw in Elizabeth Birch's attempts to engage and best biblical homophobia in its own terms, on those occasions when gay advocates have tried to talk values, they have tended to say more of the same.)

We believe a strong case can be made for linking race, sex, and sexuality. Rather than depending on dubious appeals to innate differences, we argue for the positive value of freedom with regard to social difference. By eschewing a reliance on biology, it is possible to connect rights to freedom, thereby expanding the reach of movements that are now narrowly focused on gay "rights." This move would allow us to make alliances with African American civil rights movements, which have historically worked as freedom movements, without being dependent on the problematic "like race analogy."

We make this shift by switching from the current legal framework, with its focus on nondiscrimination, to one based on the free exercise of religion promised in the First Amendment. In so doing, we are not so much interested in pursuing a strict analogy between religious and sexual identity. Rather, we are interested in opening up new political, rhetorical, and perhaps even legal perspectives and possibilities.

We want first to explore the implications of shifting from a paradigm of race to a paradigm of religion. Ultimately, though, we want to push beyond the analogical structure of either the "like race" or "like religion" framework. If, as we saw in chapter 1, sexual regulation in the United States is tied to the continuing establishment of religion in law, then sexual freedom and religious freedom are intimately tied together. And there is a multitude of other ways in which sexual freedom and the freedom to practice religion might be tied together. As Reconstructionist Rabbi and religious studies scholar Rebecca Alpert has noted, for example, the state's refusal to recognize religiously authorized gay marriages (when it recognizes other marriages performed under the same auspices) is an abrogation of the free exercise of religion.[17]

An important virtue of the paradigm shift we are advocating is that it does not force us finally to settle the question of what "causes" homosexuality. In the end, it just does not—or should not—matter how an individual came to be homosexual, any more than it matters how heterosexuals became heterosexual. Rather, homosexual life and experience are to be valued, are in fact sources of value.

The religious freedom promised in the Constitution, under the First Amendment, extends protection for religion and from it. One of the reasons religion is protected is that it is a deeply held human value, with religious commitments and the freedom of conscience and exercise necessary to make them meaningful imagined to be at the core of an individual's sense of who she or he is. The U.S. Constitution protects religion because, among other things, it recognizes that this human good is susceptible to coercion. In other words, religious identity is not understood as a natural given. Though individuals may be born into a particular faith tradition, because that is the faith practiced by their family and community, they can convert, or be coerced into converting, at some later time.[18] That an individual can be forcibly converted is among the reasons religion is protected. If "I" am to be free to practice my religion, "I" must also be free from yours. And vice versa. (Individuals can claim the right not to practice or endorse any religion at all; atheism too is supposed to be constitutionally protected as the expression of an individual's conscience.)

To say that religious identity is not encoded in the genes or passed through amniotic fluid or marked in the anterior region of the hypothalamus (some of the more popular sites for locating the "origins" of homosexuality) is not to say that individuals who identify as religious or with a particular religious tradition understand their religious identity as chosen in any simple way. The patterns of commitment that are entailed in religious identity may shift, but those patterns, which seem to touch the very core of a person—the soul even—establishing and anchoring an individual's moral center, are hardly a simple matter of "choice." Doesn't this sound an awful lot like the experience of sexual identity, which feels to many of us—homosexual or otherwise—as if it could not be otherwise, as if we could not be other than who and how we are? Recall Andrew Sullivan's words: "Homosexuality is not a behavior. It is something we are. It is a deep and integral part of our personality. It is a deep and integral part of our soul."

Religion can be an individual experience as well as a deeply social one, forging common rituals, communities of shared interpretation, and relations between individuals too. For both individuals and communities, then, religion is never a matter solely of text and belief, but crucially involves—we could even say is instantiated by—practice. In light of this, we are struck by something Sullivan's implicit analogy between homosexuality and religion leaves out: behavior, or *practice*. "Homosexuality is not a behavior," he asserts. But if homosexuality is really akin to moral personality, as Sullivan's reference to the soul suggests, how can it not involve practice?

When it comes to religion, the principles of the First Amendment do not just protect religious identity; they are supposed to protect religious practice. Moreover, as David A. J. Richards argues, the free exercise of conscience is not restricted to religiously inspired forms of conscience. Rather, the Supreme Court has "expand[ed] the constitutional concept of religion to protect conscience as such from coercion or undue burdens."[19] In practice, this means that an individual's identification and practice of the good life do not have to justify themselves in any one religion or any religion at all.

So often antigay rhetoric focuses on the malleability and "correctability" of homosexual identity (and the July 1998 advertisement discussed above is just one particularly explicit example of this tendency). But we need not restrict our responses to this rhetoric to assertions of immutability. Instead, lesbian and gay advocates could turn charges of malleability to their own advantage by taking the vulnerability of sexual identity to a logical, if unorthodox, conclusion. To require that homosexuals change or "convert" to heterosexuality in order to receive the full rights of citizenship is to compel sexual orthodoxy. And it is not simply that this sexual orthodoxy (heteronormativity) is akin to religious orthodoxy; it is an expression of a particular religious orthodoxy.

Despite the tendency—by the Supreme Court, among others—to assume and assert that moral opposition to homosexuality is a core human value, and one on which the world's religious traditions are unanimously agreed, "world religions" are not one on the subject of homosexuality. We have already noted that there is widespread disagreement between, for example, Christianity and Judaism on the morality of homosexuality. We have noted too that there are ongoing debates about homosexuality within Christian denominations and within branches of Judaism. The diversity of religious and moral views on homosexuality increases exponentially once we remember that Christianity and Judaism hardly exhaust the range of religious traditions represented in the contemporary United States. Although the fifteen organizations that sponsored the antigay ad campaign are entitled to their sectarian views on homosexuality, the principles of religious freedom enshrined in the First Amendment—disestablishment and free exercise—forbid making these narrow, sectarian views the law of the land.

The paradigm shift we are advocating—from the language of benign immutable difference (with its "can't change, can't help it" logic) to the language of values and their free exercise—could also be of benefit in the cases of race and sex. In fact, movements for civil rights or women's liberation have long connected rights to freedom. It is only with the whittling away of civil rights law since the 1980s that the focus on "benign immutable difference" has become preeminent. The gay rights movement of the last twenty years has participated in this narrowing. Alliances among these movements could be built to redress this narrowing and to resist the vision of all civil rights as "special rights," in part by regaining a focus on practice—on free exercise—in relation to race and sex, as well as sexuality. Rejecting the essentialist and racialist wager of "born that way" arguments for gay rights, we want to open up different political and rhetorical strategies that are not grounded in "benign immutable difference." After all, civil inclusion and protection from discrimination should not hinge on whether or not we were "born that way"—no matter who "we" are.

But "protection" and "rights" are not enough. A rights-based approach is too narrow to provide anything more than the type of liberal tolerance we criticized in chapter 2. By moving the ground of debate away from a constricted focus on "rights" to freedom, we hope to change a movement that, as it currently stands, is really only against something (discrimination) into one that is actively and unembarrassedly for something (freedom).

The shift from being against discrimination to being for freedom also entails a shift in focus from identity to practice. We do not want to stop at an analogy between religious and sexual identity. Rather, we want to use this analogy to jump-start more expansive considerations of not just what it means to be different, but also what it means to enact our identities differently. Tolerance extends the welcome mat to those who are different only on the condition that they set aside their difference and appear the same—like "everyone else." Instead, we hope to open social space for new forms of life that are not attached to prefixed notions of what it means to be "gay" or what it means to be "religious."

4   The Free Exercise of Sex

Rethinking sexual freedom in terms of practices rather than those of the over-arching enlightenment narratives of liberation, is a major project. Is it really possible to practice freedom in the American context? In this chapter, we turn to a constitutionally protected freedom that specifically names practice—the free exercise of religion. We are bringing together homosexuality and religion not because we want to make hard and fast claims about what it is to be religious or to be gay, but because we want to refocus public attention on practices of freedom.

At first glance, the connection that we draw between religious freedom and sexual freedom may seem strange, for at least two reasons: (1) religion is most often cited as the fundamental opponent to sexual freedom; and (2) there is not a lot of religious freedom (at least in practice) in the United States anyway. However, the freedom of religion is a potentially radical force in U.S. society. The First Amendment to the Constitution begins, "Congress shall make no law respecting an establishment of religion or prohibiting the free exercise thereof." Concerns about religion thus precede even the well-recognized freedoms of speech and of the press. There are two components that make up the religion clause: disestablishment and free exercise. As Justice Hugo Black wrote in *Everson v. Board of Education* (1947), disestablishment means "at least this: Neither a state nor the Federal Government can set up a church. Neither can pass laws which aid one religion, aid all religions, or prefer one religion over another. Neither can force nor influence a person to go or remain away from church against his will or force him to profess a belief or disbelief in any religion."[1] Free exercise means that the state should not (at least not without a compelling interest) make it difficult or impossible for any person to practice his or her religion. In other words, the state should not force any person to practice any religion, nor should the state block a person from practicing any religion.

There is much debate in legal circles over the proper relationship between disestablishment and free exercise, and even whether these two principles should be regarded as two separate clauses. We argue that the radical potential of religious freedom emerges precisely in maintaining their inseparability. In our view, there can be no real free exercise of religion without disestablishment—and vice versa.

One of the reasons that there is so little religious freedom in the United States is that we do not have genuine disestablishment; as we have seen, Christianity is the de facto established state religion. The United States practices a form of religious toleration that is not all that different from the toleration offered by the state churches of Europe, even though this limited and limiting religious toleration is what American religious freedom was supposed to overcome. Nonetheless, Christianity (specifically Protestantism) has been the religion of the land, enacted through American history in everything from prayer in public schools to the religious identifications of the president. (Controversies in 2000 over loosening these boundaries to allow for a Catholic Chaplain of the House of Representatives or a Jewish vice presidential candidate show the ways in which this de facto establishment remains in force.)[2]

In the realm of sex, we have a de facto established sexuality, heterosexuality. This is why there is a "coming out" day only for homosexuals. (Every day, it seems, is heterosexual day. Even when antigay groups stage a "coming out" event, it's a "coming out of homosexuality.") In the United States, heterosexuality is also a de jure established sexuality. Heterosexuality is privileged in federal and state laws, from immigration to taxation to healthcare. Disestablishing heterosexuality and its privileges would represent a major social transformation, a transformation that is necessary if we are to move beyond sexual toleration to sexual freedom.

As we argued in chapter 1, to the extent that state-sanctioned homophobia is, at its base, religiously motivated homophobia, the disestablishment of sexuality is not just akin to the disestablishment of religion; it cannot happen without it. But disestablishment, although a necessary condition for sexual and religious freedom, is not in and of itself sufficient. Alongside disestablishment, there must be free exercise; without it there can be neither sexual nor religious freedom.

Free exercise is important because it connects freedom with justice and with equality in particular. One of the ways in which liberal freedom can maintain structures of dominance is by proclaiming an ideal of freedom while ignoring the question of whether social conditions are such that people can actually practice this freedom. Persistent inequality of the kind that marks U.S. society means that some people can practice freedom while others most decidedly cannot. Free exercise insists on the right to practice freedom and thus demands the conditions of equality that would make this practice available to everyone.

In addition, free exercise does not depend on the boundary between public and private that protects liberal freedom. In a liberal democracy, some people are allowed to live their lives freely in both public and private; others are allowed freedom only if they keep significant aspects of their lives private and privatized; and still others (as we have seen in the case of Michael Hardwick) are not allowed even the protections of a "private life." But if "free exercise" and "democracy" are to mean anything at all, everyone must have access to life both in public and in private.

This public dimension to free exercise implies basic social freedoms like the freedom of association and freedom of assembly. In terms of sexual freedom, freedom of association and freedom of assembly would mean the claiming of public space for sexual association—and doing so on more than "gay pride" day. It is not enough to tell gay men and lesbians that they will be protected from outside interference as long as they restrict their identity-constituting and identity-confirming activities to the private sphere. Confining difference to the private sphere in no way challenges cultural dominance—instead, it extends it. This is because some people come to represent "difference" while others are the measure of us all. For example, when a heterosexual office worker puts up photographs of his wife and kids or talks to fellow workers about what he and his family did over the weekend, no one accuses him of flaunting his sexual life. But the lesbian who tells her colleagues about what she did over her weekend, and with whom, may well be accused of drawing unnecessary attention to her sex life. (In most U.S. states, she can even be fired for this "flaunting.") Although many gay men and lesbians might settle, Garbo-like, for being left alone, we advocate a more expansive view of freedom, one that contests the public-private distinction so dear to liberalism.

Being able to be "out" and not having to worry about being attacked, arrested, or fired is one version of "freedom of assembly." By being out, we do not mean elaborate gay pride parades and festivals, but rather a range of seemingly innocuous activities that are unremarkable when performed by same-race heterosexual couples—such as holding hands, making out in a car, registering at a hotel, having dinner at a candlelit restaurant. These forms of "freedom of assembly" are, in practice, routinely denied to sexual minorities. There is no short-age of public space for "heterosexual assembly." In addition to the semipublic spaces of the workplace, there are parks, restaurants, bars, courts of law, movie theaters (where heterosexuality seems to be on view no matter the genre of the movie), and so on. Furthermore, even though heterosexuality is everywhere around us, it is also so naturalized as to be virtually invisible—heterosexuals enjoy "privacy" even when they are in public. In contrast, public spaces like street corners and parks can be sites of real danger for gay men, lesbians, and other queers, who risk not just loss of livelihood, but even of life. Liberal privacy cannot even see, much less address these risks. It is precisely privacy—as it is con-structed along liberal lines—that produces these risks. This is why the notion of free exercise is so central to sexual freedom.

But what exactly does religious freedom, at least as it is laid out in the Constitu-tion, mean? Is there an impenetrable wall between church and state, or does that wall require "a few doors" (as Christian legal scholar Stephen Carter has sug-gested) for interaction between the two?[3] Does the disestablishment of religion automatically establish the ability to practice—to exercise—one's religion freely? Or are disestablishment and free exercise sometimes in contradiction with each other? All these issues have been hotly debated by politicians, scholars, and the general public. The scholarship on the religion clause is both vast and contra-dictory: for any given position taken in writing, someone else has written an-other article proclaiming the exact opposite. The jurisprudence itself has been no less contradictory. Nowhere are these contradictions more apparent than when it comes to the question of free exercise.

For example, prior to *Sherbert v. Verner* in 1963, the Court generally "distin-guished between belief and action" and held that "government may not punish citizens on account of their religious *beliefs* but may regulate religiously moti-vated *actions,* provided it has a rational basis for doing so" (emphasis added).[4]

Sherbert laid bare the stakes of separating belief and conduct in this way. The case concerned a South Carolina woman and practicing Seventh-Day Adventist, Adell Sherbert, who was fired from her job for refusing to work on Saturdays, the Sabbath day for Seventh- Day Adventists. In his summary of the sequence of events that led up to the Court challenge, conservative law and policy analyst Terry Eastland tells us that after being fired, Sherbert was "unable to find work that gave her Saturday off." She then "filed for unemployment compensation, but the state rejected her claim on grounds that she was disqualified because she had refused to accept suitable work."[5] Sherbert challenged the state's ruling, asserting that her free-exercise rights had been violated.

The Court ultimately found for Sherbert. Writing for the majority, Justice William J. Brennan, Jr., ruled that South Carolina had "force[d Sherbert] to decide between following the precepts of her religion and forfeiting [state-conferred] benefits, on the one hand, and abandoning one of the precepts of her religion in order to accept work, on the other hand." In the words of the Court, this amounted to a "Governmental imposition . . . [that put] the same kind of burden upon free exercise of religion as would a fine imposed against appellant for her Saturday worship."[6] Government could only impose such a burden, the Court reasoned, if it could demonstrate "some compelling state interest" for its policy; South Carolina had failed to do so.[7]

What came to be known as a "conduct exemption" from generally applicable secular laws was strengthened in *Wisconsin v. Yoder* some nine years later (1972). This case involved Amish parents in Wisconsin, who challenged a state law that compelled school attendance beyond the eighth grade. The Court ruled for the Amish parents and held that "a State's interest in universal education" must be balanced against the free-exercise right of the parents and their children. For Wisconsin to override this right, the Court asserted, the state had to demonstrate a "state interest of sufficient magnitude."[8]

The conduct exemption carved out in *Sherbert* and *Yoder* was short-lived: in *Employment Division v. Smith* (1990), the Court essentially reversed itself and returned to pre-1963 guidelines for infringements on religious exercise: "rational basis." *Smith* concerned two men who were fired from their jobs and subsequently denied unemployment benefits for ingesting the illegal hallucinogen peyote as part of a Native American religious ceremony. Under "rational basis," laws that burden free exercise are constitutional as long as the government can demonstrate a rational basis for its policies. This is a far looser standard of constitutional scrutiny than the "compelling state interest" guidelines and makes it much harder to challenge laws that undercut free exercise.

There are at least two reasons for these contradictory results in both the scholarship and the jurisprudence. The first problem, to which we will return, is a difficulty in holding together the two principles of the religion clause: both disestablishment and free exercise. The second, related problem is the long distance between the principles of religious freedom in the U.S. Constitution and the practice of freedom (or lack thereof) in the history of the United States. As we have seen, the understanding of America as a Christian nation contradicts the idea of religious freedom. Not only does this de facto establishment run counter to the popular conception of religious freedom in the United States, but it establishes precisely the type of "tolerance" that we criticized in chapter 2.

Religious toleration in the United States has depended on the assumption that America is, at heart, a Christian nation. Even the Supreme Court has been loath to rule against all publicly sponsored Christmas displays because to do so would be to go against practices that have long been an unreflectively central part of American national identity. The current structure of religious tolerance may not be as severe as the closeting faced by gay people. The demand on religious minorities is not the strict privatization in which "live and let live" means, "if you don't tell us you're gay we won't beat you to death." And yet, members of religious minorities often face the daily dilemma of negotiating how much of their religious "difference" they may enact in public settings. Certainly, when the Supreme Court ruled, as it did in *Goldman v. Weinberger* (1986), that Simcha Goldman, an Air Force officer and Orthodox rabbi, did not have the right to wear a yarmulke with his uniform;[9] or in *Braunfeld v. Brown* (1961), that an Orthodox Jew did not have the right to open his shop on the Christian Sabbath in violation of the state of Pennsylvania's Sunday closing laws, the Court was saying that religious difference, while tolerated in America, was not going to be treated as an equal part of American life. As we saw in *Employment Division v. Smith,* cited above, Native American religious practices were not extended First Amendment protections. More recently, at the beginning of the October term in 2001, the Court refused even to hear the appeal of a case brought by a Muslim woman whose employer would not allow her to wear a headscarf along with the company uniform while working behind the customer service desk. (She had sued under Title VII of the Civil Rights Act of 1964, which, among other things, prohibits religious discrimination in places of employment.)

Religious exemptions should increase the neutrality of the state with respect to religion such that those who do not share the religious practice of the majority have the right to equal participation in American public life. This has not been the historical effect of the religious exemption case law, however. As legal scholar Frederick Mark Gedicks reports, "No Jewish, Muslim, or Native American plaintiff has ever prevailed on a free exercise claim before the Supreme Court. Fundamentalist Christians and sects outside so-called mainline Protestantism have had only mixed success in seeking exemptions."[10] Even under the stronger constitutional standard that was in effect from 1972 to 1990, the Court could not see its way clear to ruling in favor of a free-exercise exemption that would support a non-Christian religious practice.

Still more vitally, while many Americans might want to believe that the type of lethal violence that forms the boundaries of tolerance for gay people is no longer active in relation to religious tolerance, we know that this is not actually true. Religiously motivated prejudice continues to form a tragic link in the series of violent acts that outline the limits of public life in America, from the harassment and even killing of Muslims and Sikhs after the destruction of the World Trade Center and attack on the Pentagon on September 11, 2001, to the shootings at a California Jewish Day Care Center in 1999, to the type of organized violence that killed Dr. Barnett Slepian in Buffalo, New York, in 1998. Sadly, we cannot say that religiously inspired violence is a thing of the past in the United States. Thus, to base a right to sexual freedom on a form of religious freedom that offers only a moderately better form of tolerance (if that) is hardly much of an improvement over the present situation.

The analogy between religious and sexual freedom will only work if we develop a radical version of religious freedom, one that makes room for robust pluralism both in terms of people's commitments and their practices. Thus, in making our analogy we do not depend on a stable ground of religious freedom, but hope to increase the possibilities for the free exercise of religion as well as the free exercise of sex. Moreover, our version of religious freedom stresses the freedom not to be religious as well as the freedom to be religious differently. Here we part company from both the traditional positions available to think about religious freedom. The secularists often talk about the separation of church and state, but they rarely talk about religious freedom; the religionists talk about religious freedom, but rarely do they talk about the separation of church and state.

In this way a seemingly necessary opposition is constructed. If one supports any public role for religion, one is accused of supporting religious dominance. This is not just guilt by association. Given the current constraints on public discourse, those who support religious freedom often end up building foundations for those who understand public religion to mean something like a "Christian" America. Nonetheless, because we argue for a greater public role for religious freedom *and* because we play out the rigorous demands of religious freedom, including disestablishment of government support for religion and the recognition of the right not to be religious, we believe that it is possible to distinguish our argument from that of the Christian Right. (Moreover, because we connect religious freedom to sexual freedom, we doubt that many on the religious Right will support our position.)

On the other hand, if one emphasizes the need to guard against religious dominance, one is accused of aggressively removing religion from public life and imposing secular dominance. For Gedicks, for example, any shift away from de facto establishment would result in "the replacement of public piety with public secularism" (4). Here we have one of the major issues that needs to be clarified if we are to move beyond the type of binary thinking that Gedicks's opposition between "public piety" and "public secularism" exemplifies. For many religious believers and for many advocates of secularism alike, the refusal on the part of the government to support religion is thought automatically to mandate religion's complete removal from public life. This view involves a conflation between the "state" and the "public," between government support and public life. At its base, the perspective that the only two choices are government support for religion or religion's banishment from any aspect of public life conflates secularism and disestablishment.

In contrast, we believe that it is possible to have more religious freedom (rather than simply more religion) in public as well as less government support of religion. The enforcement of the boundary between church and state does not mean that concerned citizens cannot bring their religious beliefs to their community activities and even their political activism. But religion would be restrained if these activities were performed in the name of the state—if, for example, one undertook these civic activities as a member of the school board or as the senate majority leader.

Each of the camps in this apparent opposition (secularists "versus" religionists) emphasizes one of the two principles of religious freedom (disestablishment "versus" free exercise), but not the other. We take an alternative path. In our view, there is no necessary contradiction between disestablishment and free exercise. We think that if the United States is ever to enact true religious freedom—rather than religious toleration—both principles must be applied. Given the dominance of Reformed Protestantism in our public life, there can be no genuine free exercise without disestablishment. Without disestablishment, free exercise will confuse public space with government support.

This confusion is evident in the initial version of President George W. Bush's plan for government-funded religious social service provision, and in some of the public commentary on Bush's proposals. For example, Laurie Goodstein wrote in the *New York Times* that, "The cornerstone of the president's plan is that religious programs will not be required to censor their religious teachings in order to receive government contracts. The source for this, too, is in the First Amendment—that the government shall not prohibit religious expression."[11] Such a comment misses the connections between the two principles in the First Amendment. Bush's faith-based initiatives would be reconcilable with religious freedom only if the principle of disestablishment were ignored. Certainly, in the enactment of a similar program in Texas (when Bush was governor), funding for faith-based social service programs did not enhance free exercise. For example, in one instance the state gave $8,000 to a job-training program that required Bible study and the acceptance of Jesus Christ as lord and savior, and there was no other job-training program available in the county. In this case, a claim for free exercise, which did not include disestablishment, resulted in less space for the free practice of religion, including the freedom not to be religious.

At the same time, the vision that we present is not simply a secularist vision that would make the public sphere a completely secular place, while restricting religion to the private sphere. This is what some advocates of secularism understand disestablishment to require; but in fact this version of disestablishment may actually hinder religious freedom. Because Protestant dominance habitually passes for secularism, disestablishment in and of itself can simply enact Protestantism by another name. We've already discussed this "stealth Protestantism" in thinking through the implications of *Bowers v. Hardwick* in chapter 1. In that case, the Court makes what it calls "Judaeo-Christian" tradition the baseline for secular morality and law. For other examples of the Court's upholding of specifically Christian values in the name of "the secular," we turn now to a pair of decisions related to public support for Christmas decorations, in particular "nativity scenes." In both cases, the Court voted to permit Christmas displays on publicly owned land; the Court justified its ruling with the assertion that, at least in the view of the majority, the displays were basically secular. We strongly oppose this reasoning. If "secular" is another name for a vague Christianity there is little social space to practice either the freedom to be religious differently or the freedom not to be religious at all.

In the first case, *Lynch v. Donnelly* (1984), the Court decided that the inclusion of a nativity scene in a city-owned and operated holiday display close to a downtown shopping district in Pawtucket, Rhode Island, was constitutional. The Court held that the display had a secular purpose, "to celebrate the Holiday and to depict the origins of that holiday." Its religious effects were "indirect, remote, and incidental," akin to the passive display of religious paintings. We see no such neutrality in this display. That the Christmas holiday in this depiction had been taken over by secular commercial purposes does not make it somehow "not Christian." There is no indication of the freedom to be anything other than Christian in the public life of this community. As a result, there is less, not more, space for any religious practice other than Christian practice (never mind any space for non-religious practice).

In the second case, *Allegheny County v. ACLU* (1989), there were two holiday displays in question. One was a crèche, or nativity scene, inside the County Courthouse, and the other was an outdoor display of a Christmas tree (forty feet high), a Chanukah menorah (seventeen feet high), and a sign in honor of liberty. The majority found the crèche to be a clear violation of the establishment clause. But the other display—the tree, the menorah, and the liberty sign—was allowed. There was disagreement among the concurring Justices about precisely why the display was allowable, but overall their reasoning resembled that in *Lynch*. For the majority, the combination of the different symbols in the display overshadowed any specifically religious message and made the display effectively "secular." We think the majority's reasoning is seriously flawed: just because a Christmas tree is juxtaposed with a Menorah and a sign for liberty does not mean it is no longer a religious symbol. It is a religious symbol in relation to other symbols. It does not thereby become "secular."

It would be interesting to think about this display, however, in terms of religious pluralism rather than some inchoate secularism. The relative size of the holiday display's various components all too graphically exposed the state of religious freedom in the United States: an overshadowing Christianity in conjunction with a smaller, supporting part for Judaism, a paean to liberty, and no acknowledgment of any other religious possibilities. The possibility that is hinted at, but not finally realized in this display, is that public religious expression might be multiple and that religious liberty might include the freedom not to be religious. Unfortunately, the geography of social space mapped out by the Supreme Court in *Lynch* and *Allegheny* is utterly Christian, and it is debilitating not just for religious freedom but for sexual freedom as well. One of the reasons that we argue for public space rather than simply a zone of privacy for sexual freedom is to interrupt this Christianizing map of the social. The recognition of sexual freedom as a public right is also a recognition of the right not to be Christian in the terms laid out by the dominant understanding of Christianity.

Our conception of religious freedom is based on holding together both disestablishment and free exercise. Accordingly, if we are to base a claim to sexual freedom on an analogy to religious freedom that lives up to the ideals of the First Amendment of the Constitution, then once again we would need to follow both principles. That is, we would need to disestablish sexuality (get government out of the business of regulating sexuality) and have the right to take up public space in which freely to exercise sexual difference. (This freedom to exercise sexual difference must also include the freedom to choose celibacy, but this is a far cry from abstinence-only education.)

Sexual regulation is currently enforced by a staggering number of government departments and agencies, at both the federal and local levels. When the government mandates abstinence-only sex education, defines marriage as the union of one man and one woman, creates tax incentives for married couples and their dependents, and links immigration rights to marriage, it is regulating sexuality and prescribing a particular sexual morality. The disestablishment of sexuality requires a wide-ranging reconsideration of how sex and government work. Free exercise demands that we stake out bold new terrain both in theory and in practice, for the free exercise of sex implies a series of public freedoms—freedom of association and assembly—that are standard for other areas of political life, but are currently disallowed when it comes to dissident sex.

Not all versions of religion, sex, or freedom are the same. The religion-sex analogy has recently been taken up by a number of more conservative theorists. If we want to make an intervention in the public practice of sexual freedom and we want to do so by connecting religious freedom and sexual freedom, we have to interrupt the conservative containment of First Amendment freedoms.

Exemplary of this containment are arguments from legal scholars Michael W. McConnell and Andrew Koppelman.[12] Both Koppelman and McConnell are traditional liberals in the philosophical sense, which leads them to produce more conservative readings of an analogy between the state's role toward sexuality and toward religion. Both McConnell and Koppelman take up and promote disestablishment, but not free exercise. While at first glance it may seem problematic to build an analogy to the First Amendment while leaving out one of the principles of religious freedom, it is not a surprising interpretation (as we have seen from our brief review of Supreme Court cases). McConnell and Koppelman start from the liberal premise that privatization is a means of producing "civil peace" on contentious issues. These liberal starting points, civil peace and privatization, are in fact blockages.

What do we mean by this? The predominant understanding of religious freedom in the United States depends on the privatization of religion. Religious difference is acceptable—is tolerated—if it is contained in the private sphere. This understanding of religious practice is problematic not only for many members of religious "minorities," but also for many Christians, who argue that the idea that religion is or should be only a private concern does damage to religious practice and underestimates the many benefits religion might contribute to American civic life.

Undeniably, the notion of privacy has been crucial to the development of "rights" around issues of sex and gender. It provides the basis for the right to use birth control without intervention from the state and has also provided much of the justification for women's access to abortion. But in relation to women's rights issues, privacy can also be a double-edged sword: sometimes it protects too much, laying out a zone under which various types of violence against women can take place without being treated as violence. At the same time, it also can protect too little. The patchwork of local and federal restrictions on women's access to abortion and the ongoing controversy over RU-486, the "abortion pill," demonstrate that privacy is not necessarily a bulwark against governmental interference.

If we turn our attention to issues of race and class, we can see yet more aspects of the uneven distribution and effects of privacy. Taking the example of homeless people who are denied rights to personal privacy as well as to public space, critical legal theorist Patricia J. Williams argues that privacy cannot protect those without property. Williams also carefully examines the situation of poor people, disproportionately of color, who receive state support.[13] In exchange for support from the state, meager as it may be, the recipients of "welfare" give up all kinds of privacy rights: they must accept state scrutiny in a wide variety of areas, from their personal health to their housing to their family lives.

Given all the problems of privatization and the "private sphere," why do liberal theorists continue to be invested in privacy? The liberal story behind this idea is that the institution of a secular public sphere defuses the social potency and volatility of dangerous differences like religion or gender or, in this case, sexuality, through privatization—that is, by removing these differences from public. This story covers over more than it reveals. First, in contentious areas like gender relations, it is not gender differences that are traditionally privatized, but women, and this amounts to a very different thing. Masculinity is not restricted to the private sphere, but is rather a driving force in much of U.S. public life.

Second, it doesn't produce civil peace either. Conflict is not in and of itself a problem. Public contestation does not have to be violent or even adversarial conflict, but liberalism too often remands the social differences out of which conflict might arise to the private sphere. Because these differences (and the disagreements that may arise out of them) are shut off and privatized, they cannot be publicly engaged and continue to erupt as violence.

Instead of engaging differences, the liberal arrangement produces dominance in the name of neutrality. Under such conditions, any move toward actual neutrality will feel fundamentally unfair to those whose positions of cultural privilege and dominance have never been marked as such. That is, certain social attributes and identity markers—such as maleness, heterosexuality, whiteness, or Christianness—are so taken for granted and naturalized in the United States that they function as the very measure of the human. In practice, this means that the special treatment and extraordinary access to power enjoyed by some citizens are not seen as exceptions to fair play, but as fairness itself. Thus, constant conflict is maintained, rather than ended, by a system that officially values neutrality but actually enforces hierarchy. Those who are marginalized will claim, as gay rights advocates do, that the system is unfairly biased against them. This is an accurate claim. Those who are invested in the dominance of heterosexuality will claim that any move to end marginalization is discriminatory toward the dominant group. While this claim is not accurate in the same way as the first, it does have an accuracy of feeling. If someone is told repeatedly by society that his position of dominance is an expression of fairness, that his achievements are attributable to merit and merit alone, it would be hard for him to see how ending that dominance could also be fair. When dominance is not just narrated but is actually *experienced* as fairness, the recasting of affirmative action as "reverse discrimination" and of equal rights for gays as "special rights" has its awful sense and its awful logic. These are precisely the feelings exhibited by those who argue against gay rights.

McConnell's and Koppelman's approaches to the religion-sex analogy exemplify some of these liberal problems. However, there are some important differences between these men's positions that need to be noted up front. Koppelman does lean toward advocating gay rights in a way that McConnell does not.[14] Nevertheless, for both McConnell and Koppelman, taking up the First Amendment means a focus on disestablishment alone that too often produces a false neutrality.

The phenomenon of an inequality enshrined in the language of neutrality is evident in the way that both men approach the disestablishment of sexuality. Let's follow the twists and turns of Koppelman's argument about the state's proper relationship to sexuality. At one point he says, "The proposal is that here, too, [as with religion] no faction's views are to be adopted by the state. Rather, the state would remain neutral about the moral status of homosexuality" (216). His proposal, that "no faction's views are to be adopted by the state," could not sound more neutral. And yet, by the time we get to the end of the next sentence, it becomes clear that neutrality is sought and would be enforced only when it comes to "homosexuality." This sounds good. Don't we want the state to be neutral on homosexuality? Not exactly. We want the state to be neutral about sexuality, not just homosexuality.

His argument continues: "Neutrality toward competing sexual moralities has the same advantage that . . . the principle of government neutrality toward religion has: unlike the alternatives, it is not in principle impossible that everyone could agree to it" (217). What the shift from the particular question of "homosexuality" to the universal category "sexual moralities" accomplishes is the appearance that all sexual moralities will be treated equally, that is, in a neutral manner by the state. This is the liberal trick. In fact, one sexual morality—that which privileges heterosexuality—would be enshrined in the state, while any other sexual morality—including one that is neutral between hetero- and homosexuality—would be delegitimated. This is the state promotion—establishment—of heteronormativity. This is not just the logic of Koppelman's argument, though, it is also the sexual status quo in today's United States.

By contrast, we think that state neutrality on the question of sexuality should be neutral between homosexuality and heterosexuality and not be a matter of adjudicating whether or not homosexuality is "good" or "bad." To pose the question in the way that Koppelman does, in which homosexuality is *the* question for sexual morality, is already to determine the answer. Privileging heterosexuality thus appears more neutral than neutrality itself; it has become the mirror of the moral.

Like Koppelman, McConnell slips between the disestablishment of sexuality and the disestablishment of homosexuality alone. Thus, he says, "We should recognize that the civil magistrate is no more competent a judge of the truth about *human sexuality* than about religion. Under this approach the state should impose no penalty on practices associated with or compelled by any of the various views of *homosexuality*" (215, emphasis added). He is also a firm supporter of privatization, and finds that one of the great benefits of a disestablishment approach would be the privatization of homosexuality. Meanwhile, he virtually ignores the various forms of public life that are normally part of heterosexuality.

Despite these tensions, there are points at which both Koppelman and McConnell acknowledge that the logic of their analogy requires the disestablishment of both homo- and heterosexuality. After all, if the disestablishment principle of the religious freedom clause disestablishes all religion, by analogy sexual disestablishment would require disestablishment of all sexuality. One outcome of such a claim would be to disestablish marriage. At points, Koppelman even skates close to making just such a claim. As a compromise, he suggests that it *"might"* (227, emphasis in original) be a good idea to offer marriage licenses to both hetero- and homosexual couples. McConnell, for his part, also acknowledges these logical connections between disestablishing homo- and heterosexuality and disestablishing marriage, but he cannot even accept gay marriage as a compromise.

The issue of sexual violence also troubles Koppelman. If sexuality is disestablished, he worries, can the state lawfully intervene in cases of sexual violence and abuse? This is a false worry. We would argue that the disestablishment of sexuality means that sexual conduct should not be regulated by the state, except in cases that are otherwise of concern to the state, like those of violence and abuse. Importantly, what makes, or should make, rape and other forms of sexual violence actionable is not their connection to sex or sexuality, but their enactment of violence and abridgment of consent. Sexual violence is a particular form of violence. It is not the same as battery. But it is the violence, not the sex, that justifies state intervention in the case of rape.[15]

The neutrality vis-à-vis sexuality that both men's arguments claim to espouse escapes their final grasp. Disestablishing sexuality in general, and not just homosexuality, "feels" unfair to McConnell and Koppelman, a feeling of unfairness that, once again, props up cultural dominance. Ultimately, then, their proposals would produce in the realm of sex the same type of dominance for heterosexuality that Christianity currently possesses in the realm of religion. Heteronormativity would remain the law of the land.

Contrast these suggestions with those put forward by feminist historian and long-time progressive activist Lisa Duggan. In a 1994 essay, Duggan makes the case that public policy and state institutions currently "compel, promote, or prefer inter-gender relationships over intra-gender attachments."[16] From tax relief and inheritance rights to preferential treatment in immigration cases, state-sanctioned heterosexuality confers a host of material benefits and rewards. And all this is in addition to the heterosexual couple's symbolic role as the nation's anchor, with the heterosexual family representing the body politic on a smaller scale. In response, Duggan playfully—but seriously—suggests a new disestablishmentarianism. But the "state religion" that would be disestablished is "the religion of heteronormativity" (9). The rhetorical value of such a move is that it highlights the embeddedness of heteronormativity in the state. Moreover, as Duggan also argues, the disestablishment argument stakes out some familiar ground: it exploits liberal discourse around religious tolerance and the separation of church and state. She writes, "the state may no more establish a state sexuality than a state religion, a heterosexual presumption has no more place in public than a presumption of Christianity" (9).

Ultimately, Duggan wants to use the analogy to religion in order to shift the conversation around homosexuality from a narrow focus on civil rights and benign immutable difference to the richer tradition of dissent and heterodoxy offered under the umbrella of the First Amendment's religion clause. We share

Duggan's interest in promoting conditions for sexual dissent, freedom of association, and freedom of speech, and would add to these interests freedom of assembly, the claiming of public space.

How can we open up such a space for sexual freedom? First, to repeat: to the extent that homophobia is religious domination by any other name, creating the conditions to be religious differently or, just as crucially, not to be religious at all is a necessary starting point for sexual dissent. Second, the free exercise of sex we envision is based in a robust pluralism that makes room for competing and even contradictory visions of the good life, both those that are religious and those that are not.

Sexual identity, sexual communities, and sexual practices are aspects of this good life. By making a space for values that do not depend upon any one religion or even any religion at all, perhaps we might be able to make strong claims for the value of sexual practices (including the value of chosen and committed celibacy). What do we mean by this? When it comes to homosexuality, it is not enough to say, "gay is good," even if that is a difficult enough claim to make in the current climate. We want also to say gay sex is good; it does good. Thus, instead of thinking of sexuality in general and homosexual practices in particular as objects of moral concern and regulation, we might understand sex as a rich site for the production of values. But this can only happen if religion is no longer held to be the necessary condition for all values.

The creation of more social space for sexual and religious freedom will not be the inevitable outcome of some irresistible forward movement of history. We have to forge a different kind of future, not sit and wait for it to happen. We are certainly suspicious of the Enlightenment progress narrative, which forecasts the continuous and inevitable expansion of freedom. This story is often told as the legitimating narrative of American public life. It was told in the 2000 vice presidential debates when Senator Joseph Lieberman was asked about gay marriage. Lieberman told a story in which American democracy, while overly narrow from its inception, has always expanded to include various groups of people. For him, gay marriage, while a "current and difficult" question, constitutes an issue around which such expansion should again occur. Critics of Enlightenment liberalism are suspicious of this very story because it never seems to turn out that way. Someone, it seems, is always excluded from the general public.

Liberalism's critics have argued that the reason the story never seems to reach its happy ending is because the rights and freedoms that go along with liberal citizenship are available to some people only because they are unavailable to others. This economy in which freedom for some is bought with unfreedom for others is evident in Christian conservative Gary Bauer's contribution to the debate in a *New York Times* op-ed piece, published on October 8, 2000, the week after the vice presidential debate.[17] He was disappointed with both candidates because he found them to be too liberal on the question of abortion as well as "gay rights." He would continue to support the Bush-Cheney ticket despite this betrayal because of the Republican commitment to increased military spending, tax cuts for the rich as well as the poor, and smaller government. "But," he concluded, "all of those things pale in comparison to the fundamental question of tempering our liberty with virtue."

Whose liberty is being tempered here? Not everyone's. What does Bauer's principle of tempering liberty with virtue produce in practice? A refusal of full civil rights to gay and lesbian people who want to get married (we're not anywhere close to full civil rights for those queers, homo or hetero, who think that marriage is not a fabulous institution); and a denial of a woman's right to choose. As Bauer says, "And the Republican Party must appoint judges who will respect life and insure a place at the table for all children—born and unborn" (that is, until they grow up to be women and/or homosexuals). In other words, none of the liberties that Bauer is interested in tempering is a liberty needed by Gary Bauer. Rather, for Bauer, the American liberty that is offered to some is maintained through a denial of that very liberty to others.

We do not have faith in the story of liberty's inevitable forward march. Nor do we think that freedom in the United States simply needs to be expanded; it needs to be changed. The beginning of such a change would be to connect conscience to practice. The freedom for conscientious practice, of acting on one's conscience, rather than merely having a conscience, would be a fundamental change in the American order of things. The relationship between action and free speech is so tortured precisely because American freedom was instituted to allow freedom for some and not for others. Changing the boundary line between who counts as "some" and who counts as "others" is not the type of change that we seek. Rather, we seek freedom and justice for all. Without practices of freedom, without free exercise, this refrain will remain an empty piety.

To show the difference that free exercise—Foucault's fabled "practices of freedom"—makes, we would like to turn to one final proponent of the religious freedom analogy for gay rights, legal scholar David A. J. Richards.[18] He is much more liberal in his approach than either McConnell or Koppelman. Richards would not favor only the disestablishment of homosexuality; in fact, he argues strongly against the "extreme privatization" to which homosexuality has historically been subject (192) and seeks instead public recognition of the legitimacy of gay identity and gay sexuality. We like the public dimension of Richards's argument and also appreciate the way he puts "the right to intimate life . . . on a par with the right to conscience" (175). This link is a vital one. Richards understands how moral conscience and values can arise out of the most intimate spheres of life practice, what he calls "sexual love." But he demurs from exploring the full implications of this claim. If values can arise out of sexual relations, then the usual sex-values relation is turned on its head: it's not that we need values in order to regulate sex, rather, sex is constitutive of values.

Richards speaks of the social value of the ability of persons to "explore, express, develop, revise, and sometimes change" (196) their convictions on matters of conscience. We do not disagree. However, as important as the "right to conscience" is, if conscience is cut off from the possibility of its free exercise, then sexual freedom, however nice in theory, is an empty slogan. An overemphasis on a "right to conscience" can have the unintended effect of reasserting a distinction between identity and practice, agent and act. This splitting returns us to the so-called tolerance of "love the sinner, hate the sin."

Part of the difficulty here is the way religion gets narrowed to questions of conscience, belief, or interior life. This is an odd way of conceiving what religion is, but it is also the dominant American understanding of religion. If you begin the religion-sexuality analogy with this inward-looking view of religion, then sexuality is correspondingly narrowed to a matter of interiority, "being" not "doing." But religion is no more reducible to what an individual believes than sexuality is contained by what an individual "is." There must be space for practice, for enactment, in both individual and communal contexts. Where both religion and sex are concerned, performance is constitutive of identity. It is a peculiarly Christian—and Reformed Protestant—tendency to make belief the warp and woof of religiosity. For many other religions, and even for some Protestant denominations, practice is the definitive element.

We need a way to think about the religion-sexuality relationship that makes a strong claim for the value of sexual practice and for the mutual constitution of identity and act. And we must do so without making the value of sex depend upon the ideology of romantic love. Richards refers to "sexual love" and "sexual intimacy" and praises them as sources of moral value. This is all well and good, but we would argue equally for the public importance of a wide array of consensual sexual practices, including those that are not related to either love or intimacy. The value of sex—its value-making capacity—does not rise and fall on whether or not sexual acts are also acts of love.

5   Valuing Sex

What does it mean to take sex seriously as a site for the production of values? Sexual relations are human relations, and the activity of making sex forges these relations. We use the language of "making sex" (rather than "making love") because, as we stated in the previous chapter, we don't think that the value of sex necessarily depends upon whether the people involved are in love. But even more fundamentally, we believe that there is no one act or set of acts that constitutes "sex"—there are as many ways to make sex as there are people. "Making sex" better captures the agency and the imagination involved in sexual relations than does the term "having sex." This agency is ethical agency, which involves how we relate to each other—sexually and otherwise.

Throughout this book we've been pursuing some deeply counterintuitive ideas about the role of religion in American public life, the insufficiency of tolerance as a basis for democratic differences, and the mutual entailment of religious and sexual freedom. All these claims make possible alternative understandings of sex, ethics, and freedom. In turn, these alternative understandings make possible new forms of social life. This is not newness for the sake of newness, but change for the sake of making a variety of subject positions more inhabitable, more survivable, than they currently are. We are thinking about the situation of homosexuals and other sexual dissidents certainly, but we are also cognizant of the high costs that can come with inhabiting even the most traditional of "nuclear families."

As we've argued, it's difficult in America to produce a language of values (never mind sexual values) that isn't framed in religious and, particularly, in Christian terms. This produces a situation in which values translate as Christianity, and vice versa. Here is another example of this American common sense at work. In October 2001, as their patriotic response to the September 11 attacks on the World Trade Center and the Pentagon, the city council of Ringgold, Georgia, voted unanimously to post the Ten Commandments and the Lord's Prayer at city hall—along the corridors outside the courtroom ("All Things Considered," NPR, October 16, 2001). Anticipating challenges from the American Civil Liberties Union (ACLU) and other civil libertarians, the city decided to hang up another plaque, one that would represent an alternative, nonreligious point of view. (Evidently, the religious point of view could be crystallized in the Ten Commandments and Lord's Prayer alone.) The plaque representing the moral alternative to religion was blank. In Ringgold's public imagination, religious values are "Judaeo-Christian values," and non–Judaeo-Christian values are formless, without content, empty. Are these the only choices: religious values or no values?

If it's difficult for many Americans to imagine moral possibilities that are not ultimately grounded in religious claims, this problem becomes even more acute when it comes to sex. When sex is construed as the problem and religion as the solution, there is little room to think about sex itself as a kind of ethical relation and still less room to think about sex as a practice of freedom. Freedom is supposed to be the first principle of American democracy. But the free exercise of sex is virtually unthinkable. When sexual freedom is contemplated it raises the specter of licentiousness, not liberty. Sex seems to be the one area in American life where we will not let freedom reign and where the mere suggestion of freedom seems nonsensical at best and highly immoral at worst. Connecting sexual freedom to religious freedom, as we are proposing, may seem like an impossible—to some, even an offensive—undertaking.

Objections to our argument can come from two different directions. One set of objections, commonly heard in contemporary public discourse, comes from those (usually sexual conservatives) who think that sexuality requires regulation and that such regulation is a moral imperative. Another set of objections comes from progressives who worry that any use of the language of values will necessarily result in some form of coercive regulation. Perhaps surprisingly, our response to these two sets of critics is similar: Not all uses of the language of values are the same; not all ethics are geared toward regulation.

Conservatives are often used to rattling off a litany of harms that are attendant to sexual freedom (harms that could be ascribed equally to heterosexuality and homosexuality). Yet, in this honor roll of horrors, conservatives rarely offer any explanation as to why sexual freedom is the height of immorality and selfishness, while other types of freedom—political and economic freedom, for example, or freedom of speech and thought—are not only expressions of high moral principles, but are, in fact, the central values of the American nation. Conservatives point to the putative consequences of sexual freedom: unwanted pregnancy, sexually transmitted disease, AIDS, broken homes, children without fathers (and from there it is a short slide to poverty and crime). Compare this to discussions of economic and political freedom: here, any argument about consequences is deemed irrelevant. For example, freedom of speech is so important, conservatives argue, that it must be protected regardless of consequences (unless, of course, the speech in question is *sexual speech*). Even hate speech must be protected, regardless of the harm inflicted on individuals or the damage done to the community as a whole.[1]

If we are willing to accept the consequences when it comes to some freedoms, what makes sex such a different case? Why, for example, is sexual speech an exception to the otherwise free speech absolutism of many social conservatives? The conservative response to this challenge usually takes some form of the following: sex is too trivial to warrant such risk taking. To pursue sexual freedom is mere self-indulgence. And yet, as we saw in Congress's response to President Clinton's affair with Monica Lewinsky, "the wrong kind" of sex was also considered important enough to impeach the president, and the issues of sexual respectability raised by proponents of impeachment were important enough to remain at the center of the 2000 presidential campaigns. Here we have one of the central contradictions of American thinking about sex. Sex is *both* frivolous, a "merely" private concern, *and* central to American public life.

We believe that sexual freedom is not a frivolous question. Like the other American freedoms (freedom of conscience and freedom of speech), sexual freedom is a value worth protecting. Sexual freedom is the freedom to form human relationships. This is why sexual freedom should not be dismissed as mere self-indulgence, for which it is often mistaken.

In addition to the accusation of frivolousness, those who advocate sexual freedom must confront the accusation of "moral relativism," never a term of approbation. Those who are labeled "moral relativists" generally believe that standards of good and bad behavior are not universal principles, but emerge out of specific historical and cultural contexts or environments. However, they are often understood to be saying: anything goes, everyone and anyone can determine what is good or bad, moral and immoral, for him or herself, and no one is in a position to make judgments about anyone else's behavior.

As with the false choice between religious values or no values, this understanding of what it means to see morality as "relative" often sets up a misleading, and ultimately unhelpful, dichotomy between moral relativism and moral absolutism. It is misleading in part because absolutist morality is never as absolute as its invocation sounds. Most people would acknowledge, for example, that there are times when moral principles, including absolute moral principles, come into conflict. This conflict sometimes leads to the abridgment of one or another of these (supposedly absolute) moral principles.

In fact, these principles are often abridged for a variety of reasons. Take the basic moral prohibition against killing other human beings, for example. This would seem to be the most fundamental of absolute moral principles, and yet organized killing in the form of war is also common across the world. While there are those who maintain that this principle is unimpeachable and refuse any type of killing, the vast majority of Americans are willing to abridge this principle in the case of war and often with regard to capital punishment. William Bennett, the virtual dean of the new conservative morality, argues that war itself is a moral crucible, the place where the highest moral virtues are forged, and those who oppose war, like the participants in the sixties and seventies U.S. antiwar movement, are harbingers of moral decay.[a]

Absolutist morality has difficulty recognizing the type of moral complexity in which moral principles like that against killing are abrogated for various reasons or in which moral principles and moral struggles are themselves complex. In actual experience, many people's mistrust of absolutist morality comes from the fact that life rarely seems to fit into such simple—yes or no, absolutely good, absolutely bad—terms. Nevertheless, despite this gut-level feeling that our experiences do not square with absolutist approaches, people often feel at a loss for other ways of thinking about and articulating moral quandaries.

If there is not a single morality by which to judge all moral positions, then we are supposedly left in a position in which it is impossible to distinguish between positions at all. From the perspective of an absolutist morality, then, relative or relativist morality is tantamount to no morality. This is an unfortunate formulation of moral possibilities, however, because it leaves us without the moral language to confront our social world. If moral absolutism is insufficient in relation to the world in which we live, then we need to develop the moral language to distinguish between moral situations despite their complications.

Such a language would be able to acknowledge moral differences and to provide a means for working with these differences. Obviously, a moral position that recognizes these different moralities can be called "relativist," but this relativism need not be a loss in moral possibility. Rather, to be relative to something is to be *in relation to it*. Moral differences are not formed in a vacuum, they are formed in social relations. The challenge of democracy is the challenge of public engagement with moral differences.[3]

Here moral differences are not restricted to the private sphere, they are publicly engaged. This is a robust pluralism. For those who fear that there is a loss here (of social cohesion in the move from a liberal pluralism that depends upon the privatization of differences to a robust pluralism that recognizes public differences) we should remember that, in fact, moral differences have long been part of American public life. The idea that there is a single morality that guides American life is as misleading as the idea of absolutist morality. The United States has never depended solely on the objective application of a single, agreed upon moral system. We have always worked out moral meanings through the history of democratic engagement.

The slippage from the accusation of moral relativism to the accusation of amorality makes invisible the fact that many of the new social movements that are the supposed purveyors of moral relativism have been organized around moral notions, including moral notions of freedom: from freedom riders in the civil rights movement to women's and gay liberation, the moral claims of freedom have been central in U.S. social movements. This is not surprising given the centrality of freedom to American politics, but freedom is one of the most complicated moral concepts in American history.

As historian Eric Foner has carefully traced in *The Story of American Freedom*, because freedom has been such an organizing principle in American politics, it has also carried many different meanings—meanings that have been contested time and again in American history:

> The very universality of the language of freedom camouflages a host of divergent connotations and applications. It is pointless to attempt to identify a single "real" meaning against which others are to be judged. Rather than seeing freedom as a fixed category or predetermined concept, I view it as an "essentially contested concept," one that by its very nature is the subject of disagreement. Use of such a concept automatically presupposes an ongoing dialogue with other, competing meanings.[4]

Freedom, from this perspective, is ethically valuable because it opens the door to democratic contestation. Such possibilities will be underrealized, however, unless we develop richer vocabularies for discussing values and moral differences.

Although there is an important history of progressive social movements actively and explicitly struggling with the question of freedom and values, nonetheless many progressive intellectuals and activists have become suspicious of any use of moral language at all. These progressives are concerned about the ways in which moral language can be used as a club in public discourse to shut down opposing viewpoints and enforce social control. Although there may be good reasons for progressives to be cautious in this regard, it has not been so easy to forgo moral language altogether. Refusing to speak in moral terms does not necessarily remove one from the moral fray. Certainly, conservatives continue to use moral arguments to castigate progressives on a range of social issues, and it is not as if a refusal to talk values has exempted progressives or even liberals from such attacks. Cautioning against the use of moral language can result in not having it when you most need it. Our project is to develop other ways to talk about values.

This project takes on special urgency where sex and sexual regulation are concerned. Many sex radicals worry that moral language about sexuality inevitably leads to sexual regulation. They point out that how one has sex is so often taken to be a barometer of whether one has values. Anthropologist Gayle Rubin, for example, argues that sexual acts have been "burdened with an excess of significance."[5] In this situation, where sex is supercharged with moral meaning, Rubin and others have responded by seeking to separate sex from any moral discourse.

One of the reasons that advocates like Rubin work to remove sexual desire from moral discourse is that they are concerned that morality is always, at least in the last case analysis, geared toward regulation. Indeed, Rubin makes the broader and not inaccurate point that sexual ethics has historically been the means not of establishing justice, but of creating social hierarchies. In this system of value, moral arguments do not establish new ethics or even new ethical positions, but merely redraw social hierarchies based on sexual preference. While there have been variations in the historical form that moral hierarchies around sex have taken—for example, oral sex between men and women has sometimes moved from being morally taboo (even legally proscribed) to being less worthy of either moral or legal sanction—rarely are such hierarchies overturned altogether. These changes in the evaluations of sexual acts can happen because, ultimately, there is no strong basis for moral judgment. Instead, Rubin argues, there is a customary evaluation that establishes its authority by distinguishing itself from a despised sexuality. As in: "We" know heterosexuality to be good, because homosexuality is bad. Each claim that "we are good because others are bad" reassures those who want the line to be drawn somewhere.

Conservatives in the United States, for instance, still want to say that only monogamous heterosexuality in marriage is an appropriate sexual morality. In contrast, for the majority of Americans there is now some greater openness about morally acceptable sexuality. But the circle of those sexual acts that are included in the realm of acceptability is still small. Moreover, the main impetus of much of the movement for lesbian and gay rights has been to move homosexual acts in monogamous relationships into this "charmed circle," to use Rubin's term (13), rather than to institute a widespread sexual justice for all. Monogamous gays thus invoke a sexual morality that aligns them with heterosexual monogamy and defines promiscuous gays as the moral problem. Another version of this strategy is when homosexuals claim that the gender of sexual partners should not be a moral issue, but the type of sex act should be. They accordingly define themselves as "just like" good heterosexuals and against those (whether hetero- or homosexual) who practice S/M, or sadomasochism, for example. As we can see, most of the claims for the moral rightness of one group are established by naming some other group—the "promiscuous," the "sadomasochists"—as the moral problem. Moral acceptance of any particular sex act is built on the moral denigration of others, and Rubin considers this system to be socially unjust and morally bankrupt.

Rather than conceptualizing sexual preferences as a moral issue, Rubin counters by proposing that differences in sexual taste are reflective of what she terms "benign sexual variation." "One of the most tenacious ideas about sex," she writes, "is that there is one best way to do it, and that everyone else should do it that way. Most people find it difficult to grasp that whatever they like to do sexually will be thoroughly repulsive to someone else, and that whatever repels them sexually will be the most treasured delight of someone, somewhere" (15). Feminist Carole Vance makes a similar point when she argues that the variety of human sexual interest follows a "one-third rule." Of those who view any given sexual image, "one-third will find it disgusting, one-third will find it ridiculous, and one-third will find it hot."[6]

So, when it comes to sex, "people are different from each other."[7] Moreover, the ways in which they are different far exceed the neat, or supposedly neat, categories of "homosexual" and "heterosexual." This variation in the ways in which people experience sex, in what they find repulsive and pleasurable, is not, or should not be, a matter for moral concern. Nonetheless, time and again sexual preferences or tastes have become the object of intense moral scrutiny and sanction. To counter the breathtaking moral terms in which sex and especially differences in sexual taste are so often cast, Rubin (along with other theorists like David M. Halperin) has proposed that sexual taste, like taste in food, should be considered a nonmoral—not immoral or amoral, but nonmoral—question of human difference. We don't make moral judgments about whether individuals in U.S. society prefer spicy or mild food; similarly we should not make judgments about whether individuals prefer spicy or mild sex.

Of course, as soon as one says that sexual appetite is an appetite akin to that for food, the objection arises, but what if one's sexual appetites just happen to include a desire for sex with children? We take child sexual abuse seriously, but this question is in many ways misleading. It does not directly address child abuse even as it short-circuits any discussion of the wide variety of human sexual interests that have nothing to do with children. There is no surer way to block substantive discussions about sexuality than to invoke threats to children. Say "homosexual" and "child" anywhere close to the same sentence, and the specter of the predatory homosexual (read "pedophile") is not long to follow.

This is a false stereotype. Those who identify as "heterosexual" are statistically much more likely to abuse children sexually than are those who identify as "homosexual." According to statistics published by the U.S. Department of Health and Human Services, the most common perpetrators of child sexual abuse are the male parents of the children (in other words, men who are actively heterosexual).[8] But—as with homophobic discourse more generally—the power of this stereotype often exceeds attempts to debunk it. Thus, this stereotype can be effectively deployed so that it ends political debate about sexual practices among adults even as it distracts from discussion of the most common forms of child sexual abuse.

We believe strongly that our society should work to prevent child abuse as well as to realize sexual justice. But promoting sexual conservatism among adults does not address the problem. In fact, as we sadly saw in the recent scandal about child sex abuse in the Catholic Church, those who promote sexual conservatism—in this case members of the Catholic hierarchy—may be the very same persons who perpetrate, or protect those who perpetrate, child sexual abuse. We need, then, to disentangle the question of child abuse and adult sexuality not simply as a step toward instantiating sexual freedom for adults, but also because making this distinction will allow society more clearly to focus on and prevent child sexual abuse.

How do these concerns square with our apparent endorsement of an analogy between sexual tastes and food preferences? At first glance, the suggestion that sexual tastes are akin to other bodily aptitudes and appetites may appear to cut sexuality off altogether from any public dimension. After all, the analogy seems to suggest that sex, like food, is merely a question of personal taste. Several things need to be said here. First, within numerous religious and nonreligious worldviews, food can be a profoundly moral issue: from the kosher rules of different branches of Judaism, to Hinduism's proscriptions on killing and eating cows, to the meatless Fridays of Roman Catholicism's Lent, to the strong moral feelings that ground much vegetarian practice. For some people and communities, then, food is a moral issue, but even within such communities there can be a diversity of moral views and ethical practices. (Some vegetarians, for example, avoid eating not just meat and fish, but any animal-related product, including eggs and dairy products. Other vegetarians, by contrast, will eat eggs and dairy.) Moreover, even for those for whom food does raise moral issues, not every meal they take is invested with the same degree of heightened moral concern. The Catholic who does not eat meat on Lenten Fridays may feel no moral compunction against eating meat any other Friday of the year. (Sometimes a roast beef sandwich is just a roast beef sandwich.) In the United States, the government remains neutral (or is supposed to) with respect to these different religious and moral positions on diet; it does not, for example, compel vegetarians to choose between eating meat and not eating at all.

Our second reason for finding the food-sex analogy helpful has to do with the issue of privacy. Whether viewed as a matter of moral concern or not, food and the many practices involved with it (such as cooking and eating) are certainly not restricted to "the private." People customarily buy and eat food in public—without being arrested.

Public recognition of benign sexual variation as a human good is absolutely vital, and it is certainly an improvement over assertions of "benign immutable difference." In the modern period, the major means for separating sex from ethics is the privatization that we have criticized throughout this book. It is tempting to argue that sex is a purely personal affair and that it need not be a matter of public moral concern. This line of thought, which is all about drawing boundaries between sites of appropriate state concern and regulation on one side, and zones free of interference on the other, fits well with liberalism's distinction between public and private spheres. However, such privatization does not expand the possibilities for free exercise. Additionally, treating sex as a purely private issue gets in the way of a richer public discussion about sex and ethics. By focusing on privacy, we lose a major strategic possibility for talking about and revaluing sex.

When faced with morally regulating discourse about sexuality, we should respond by pointing out that sex is overburdened as a site of anxiety. How people engage in sexual activity does not make or break the economy or the nation.

Much of what passes for moral discourse about sex is misplaced. We want to re-move questions of sexual taste from moral discourse because it doesn't really matter whether people find a sexual image compelling, disgusting, or humorous. Significantly, this does not have to mean segregating sex from ethics.

On the one hand, then, sexual preferences and "tastes" ought be no more and no less morally loaded than the kinds of food an individual prefers and the social contexts in which he or she likes to enjoy them (for example, alone, in a couple, or in a larger group). On the other hand, we advocate sexual freedom as a positive value because we don't think that sexual variation is acceptable only if it is "benign," in the sense of being nonmoral. In democratic societies freedom is not just applicable to those forms of human variation that can be successfully labeled nonmoral and contained in the private sphere. Rather, democracy is founded on freedom because it is supposed to allow for different views of the good life, in other words, for moral variation. These moral differences are fully public; they are, in fact, the substance of democracy.

Many gay male and lesbian social theorists and activists have valued sex precisely for its ability to remake social relations, what—using slightly different terms—we would even call the "value-making" capacity of sex.[9] Thus, even as we vigorously contest the terms in which opponents of homosexuality condemn homosexual sex and the "homosexual lifestyle," we do not necessarily reject any and all connections between sex and ethics. Instead, we want to remake these sexual and ethical relations.

Boldly put, we do not think we should have to choose between understand-ing and experiencing sex as one bodily pleasure among others and understanding and experiencing sex as a morally significant relation with others. In our view, sex can be both these things (even if it's not always both at once). We don't have to accept the current terms of public moral discourse about sex and then choose ei-ther bad morals or no morals. In thinking about sexual ethics, then, we need not only to question sex, but also to question ethics.

Michel Foucault is most often thought of in the United States as a theorist of "sexuality." But in his later work, he made a significant turn toward rethinking ethics. Foucault takes an approach to the sex-values question that is related to Rubin's, but is also importantly different:

> For centuries we have been convinced that between our ethics, our personal ethics, our everyday life, and the great political and social and economic structures, there were analytic relations, and that we couldn't change anything, for instance, in our sex life or our family life, without ruining our economy, our democracy and so on. I think we have to get rid of this idea of an analytical or necessary link between ethics and other social or economic or political structures.[10]

Here Foucault argues that there is no direct link between the ethics of personal relations, including sexual relations, and economics and politics. At one level, this argument is both powerful and necessary. What, for example, does it really mean to say, "Homosexuality can end Western civilization as we know it"? (This question is particularly specious given that same-sex acts seem to have consistently been part—sometimes an idealized and sometimes a reviled part—of Western civilization.)

One of the reasons that it seems like sex is implicated in economics and politics is the way we have bundled a number of social relations into sex. We often connect sex with money matters, for example; couples are assumed to mix their financial concerns. Much legal regulation of sexuality in the form of marriage is about money. When divorcing couples end up in court, it is often because they cannot come to terms with regard to their financial assets. Analogously, one of the ways in which persons can establish their domestic partnership for the sake of "domestic partners' benefits" is to show that their finances are commingled. And what of these domestic partners' "benefits"? Why does a sexual relationship, albeit one that also implicates finances, entitle one to benefits like health insurance? On the face of it, there certainly is no direct connection between making sex with someone and being able to offer that person health insurance.

Foucault suggests that this bundling is not necessary. Rather, it is a remainder of a set of social choices that were not unavoidable and, thus, could—and can still—be changed. For example, the need for health insurance as a benefit of domestic partnership is related to two separate problems. First, the decision to place the burden for the expense of healthcare on employers is a social choice, not a necessity. Not all nations place such burdens on employers. Paying for healthcare in this fashion has proven costly for American business and has meant that many Americans have access to healthcare only through their spouses, while many Americans do not have access to healthcare at all. Second, even given a conservative, employer-based system of paying for healthcare, why tie access to health insurance to a presumptively sexual relationship? If not everyone in society is employed at a level that allows for health benefits, why should some people be able to provide their sexual partners with health insurance? If the stated reason is the support of families, then why not make it possible to name any single family member? Why not an aging parent or a sibling who works only part time and so does not qualify under most employers' health plans? Foucault's point is that one reason we think that so much rides on sexual relations is that we have chosen to make it so. The inference here is that we can also make it otherwise and change our social relations—for the better.

We need to disaggregate, or unbundle, the set of social goods currently brought together under the rubric of sex and marriage (or even domestic partnership). This insight has important ramifications for our discussion of the interplay between disestablishment and free exercise. Under current social arrangements we cannot freely practice sex, because we have established it as central to social relations that have no necessary connection to sex: emotional ties, raising and caring for children, living arrangements, financial responsibility.

Although many people experience these intimacies as linked to sex, it is important to recognize that not everybody wants to have all these intimacies in the same place. Some people, for instance, may forge their most central intimacies in nonsexual relationships; although they may take lovers, their enduring emotional support comes through their friendship circles. Perhaps they have even decided to coparent with someone who is not, and never was, a sexual partner. And yet, in its privileging of marriage and the marital couple, the state enforces a particular way of doing and experiencing these important intimacies. Think, for example, of the myriad legal and social privileges extended to married couples. Feminist law professors Paula Ettelbrick and Nan Hunter, among others, point out that marriage establishes a next-of-kin relationship and thus founds a whole series of interlocking legal rights that include reduced tax liability; inheritance rights; survivor's benefits upon death of a spouse; ongoing legal ties to children when one of the parents has died; and special consideration in immigration cases (marriage to an American citizen generally gives a foreigner right to U.S. residency).[11] Marriage effectively creates a two-tier system that allows the state to regulate relationships. Why should anyone have to submit her or his consensual relationships to the state for either recognition or regulation? Why should some consensual ways of doing intimacy and family get the stamp of state approval and others not?[12]

As Foucault powerfully states:

We live in a relational world that institutions have considerably impoverished. Society and the institutions which frame it has limited the possibility of relationships because a rich relational world would be very complex to manage. . . . In effect, we live in a legal, social, and institutional world where the only relations possible are extremely few, extremely simplified, and extremely poor. There is, of course, the fundamental relation of marriage, and the relations of family, but how many other relations should exist![13]

If Foucault helpfully pushes us to disaggregate the social relations we customarily bundle into sex, he is also making a deeper point about ethics. He is concerned that our ethical understandings are bound up precisely in relations that are not necessarily ethical, but that are socially functional. Foucault wants to disentangle our everyday life from the type of ethics and regulation, including sexual regulation, that reinforces systems of power. The idea that "homosexuality can end Western civilization as we know it" is based not on the immediate effects of any given sexual act, but on the belief that sexual regulation is necessary to ethical existence itself. Amazingly, sex—rather than economics or politics—is the caliber of social ethics. (Does a society have ethics? Just look at its sex.)

Rubin worries over this problem too, but Foucault's approach is somewhat different in that he doesn't want to remove sex from ethics completely. Rather, he wants to change our ethical relations.[14] Because of our own critique of attempts to privatize sex, we too are hesitant simply to remove sex from the realm of ethics. Foucault treads close to this privatization when he says we should remove our "*personal* ethics, our *everyday* lives" (emphasis added) "from other social or economic or political structures."[15] It is important not to confuse unbundling the set of relations that currently go along with sexual relations, especially state-sponsored sexual relations (otherwise known as marriage), with privatizing any or all of those relations. Nor is this a matter of expanding the franchise of state-sponsored marriage to those who cannot currently marry. To repeat: the state should not and need not be in the business of endorsing any particular familial form (and then calling it "the family"). The state should be neutral with regard to familial form. However, this disestablishment in no way requires the state to withdraw from its important supporting role in providing the necessary means of sustenance—healthcare, child care,

ensuring a living wage, adequate housing—for its citizens. All these are the necessary prerequisites for freedom, including the freedom to form intimate relations of our own choosing.

Thus, we want to remove sex from its burden of oversignification, without
turning toward the privatization of sex. We focus on free exercise, on public
practices of freedom, rather than on the privatized freedom of choice offered by
political liberalism and the market. When practices of freedom are emphasized,
ethics is not just about the regulation of relationships or the repression of desires
or the disciplines of the body; ethics is also about the social relations that can be
generated out of interaction. Ethics becomes a project of imagining and enacting forms of life, a project that is not solitary or restricted to a zone of privacy.
Sexual relations as ethical relations should be part of public contestation. But the
focus of this contestation should be what freedom and free exercise mean, not
whether sex is a proper subject of freedom; in a democratic system, all human
relations, including sexual relations, should be the subject of freedom.

One of the reasons to protect and promote freedom is that freedom allows
for the development of moral alternatives. These alternatives are part of the social good that freedom brings into the world and can help realize the "rich relational world" dreamed of by Foucault.

Many gay and lesbian social theorists and activists as well as numerous feminist and womanist critics have understood that sex, precisely because it is embedded in interpersonal relations, can help constitute new forms of social life.
Paradoxically, then, the extraordinary moral pressure placed on sex—up to and
including the fact that this pressure bears down especially hard on those whose
sexual practices fall outside the "charmed circle" of a monogamous and reproductive heterosexuality—may also offer opportunities for reimagining the good
life and reshaping social relations. This paradox helps explain why some of the
same people who are leery of moralizing about sex also want to articulate sex's
values.

In saying this, we are building on a rich tradition of community formation and self-making elaborated in and by gay and lesbian communities. For example, although gay men are often stigmatized in the popular imagination for their "promiscuity" and "public sex," many gay male theorists have passionately defended both and in decidedly ethical terms. Activist and writer Michael Bronski has even suggested that what worries so many opponents of gay rights is less that heterosexuals will be recruited into "homosexual *sexual* activity" than that heterosexuals "will be drawn into the more flexible norms that gay people, excluded from social structures created by heterosexuality, have created for their own lives."[16] Bronski and others have argued that dissident—or "queer"—sexual practices have been creative forces for constructing new cultural forms, new patterns of relations with one another as well as responsibility for and toward one another.[17]

In his historical research, Allan Bérubé has charted the important role played by bathhouses (and other quasi-public sites in which men had sex with other men) in the development of gay identity and community. He suggests that "by using the openly gay bathhouses," gay men learned not only to enjoy having sex with other men but also to love, care for, other men. He continues, "At a time when no one was saying 'gay is good,' the creation of an institution in which gay men were encouraged to appreciate each other was a major step towards gay pride."[18] In Bérubé's analysis, then, the moral good of sexual pleasure became a site for the development of another moral good: ties of affect, care, and affirmation.

A willingness to take responsibility for each other, which can grow out of sexual relations, has certainly been on view in both gay and lesbian responses to HIV and AIDS. In the face of prolonged government indifference, gay men, lesbians, and their allies came together in the early 1980s to create community-based organizations across the country, such as New York City's Gay Men's Health Crisis, that would attend to the particular health and spiritual needs of gay men and others living with AIDS. They did so at a time when the government refused to recognize the devastating effect HIV and AIDS were having on gay men. Although sexual conservatives were wont to blame gay men for their plight—gay men had brought the disease on themselves and now must pay with their lives, conservatives thundered—gay sexual communities and networks actually enabled the development of safer sex education programs and local healthcare initiatives. As cultural critic and AIDS activist Douglas Crimp writes (and his is a profound challenge to those sexual conservatives, heterosexual and gay, who would dismiss out of hand the value of gay male sexual communities), it is these social networks that have allowed gay men to survive not just in the face of a devastating disease and indifferent state, but in the face also of a hostile world that devalues whom and how we love.[19] Gay men knew how to reach out to each other; the bathhouses and bars that were the site of their sexual networks also became places to distribute safer sex information and organize politically.

Lesbian sexual and social networks too have provided occasions for creating new cultural forms. With long-time lesbian activist and public intellectual Amber Hollibaugh, though, we must be careful not to assume that the "history of lesbian struggles" or the forms of lesbian sexual networks will be the same as gay mens'.[20] Gender and gender-based oppression have been crucial factors in the development of lesbian sexual ethics. For many reasons, including ideological associations between women and "the private sphere," and the fact that sexuality for women has often been marked out as a site of lurking danger rather than potential pleasure, historically there have not been the same opportunities for lesbians to develop the sort of public and quasi-public sexual institutions that characterize gay male sexual culture. Nonetheless, despite and perhaps in some sense because of material constraints on their public assembly, lesbians have forged fresh possibilities for doing intimacies, sexual and otherwise. For example, social historians Elizabeth Lapovsky Kennedy and Madeline D. Davis have documented the rich communities that lesbians developed in the working-class culture of 1950s Buffalo, New York.[21] The histories of such communities are complicated. But the accounts offered by Kennedy and Davis, along with the moving autobiographical testimony of poet and activist Audre Lorde, who writes about New York City, also show us that these communities produced alternative practices of sex and gender that offered some safety and support in the face of repressive gender, sexual, racial, and class norms.[22]

Additionally, lesbian sexual ethics has developed alternative ways of doing kinship. Many lesbians, for example, maintain close ties to former lovers. They do not understand the formation of a new sexual and romantic partnership, even a monogamous one, to require jettisoning others with whom they have an important history of connection, sexual and affective. Here, we can see not only that sexual intimacy can lead to other kinds of intimacy, but that these other important intimacies—of friendship and companionship—are not necessarily broken when a sexual relationship ends. Lesbian affinities of this kind become the ground for alternative ways of thinking about and doing family ties. Importantly, these alternative practices of sexual ethics, familial form, and emotional connection need not be available only to lesbians—or gay men, for that matter.

If lesbian or gay "does" good, then the good it performs is not for homosexuals alone. Rather, the alternative values developed in lesbian and gay sexual communities offer all of us a deeply ethical vision of the work sex can do to open up new horizons of possibility between people.[23] What is at stake here is nothing less than what kind of social world, what kind of America, we wish to create and inhabit. Sexual relations are part of this reimagination of the possible.

Conclusion

Open Endings, Dreaming America

The tolerance of "love the sinner, hate the sin" is antidemocratic. Democracy has to mean more than coercive homogeneity. For those who are the measure of the norm there's no great problem because their values form the center of public life and national identity; but for those who are in any way different from this dominant identity—whether in terms of race, ethnicity, gender, sexuality, class, physical ability, religion, citizenship, politics, or ethics (in other words, a lot of people)—to be included in the dream of America requires setting aside, hiding, or bracketing what makes them different in the first place. Likeness may be a criterion for membership in private organizations, but it can never be a requirement of belonging in a democracy. How then to resist and challenge exclusion and at the same time change the terms of inclusion? Is it possible to build a public that allows for robust contestation and radical pluralism, rather than one split by divisions between those who are the same and those who are different?

In order to consider these questions, we must think about sex, and we must think about sex differently. Relatedly, because sex is so peculiarly linked to religion in America, to think about sex differently mandates thinking about religion differently.

As we argue in the first half of the book: If (1) American national identity is dependent upon a sense of moral purpose, and (2) moral sensibilities are collapsed into religious belief, and (3) sexual behavior is made out to be the last and best measure of the moral, then (4) religiously derived sexual regulation plays a formative role in our national life. Nowhere is this sexual regulation made more clear than in the range of federal and state laws and policies directed at homosexuality. State laws criminalizing consensual sex between persons of the same sex are held to be constitutional, as is discrimination against homosexuals in quasi-public organizations like the Boy Scouts, as is the restriction on even speaking homosexuality in the military, as is the refusal to grant gay people the rights and privileges of marriage.

In the second half of the book, we ask: How could it be otherwise? That is, if the first half of the book has laid out the problems that we face and their context, in the second we offer alternative visions for politics and ethics. We seek to reanimate the possibilities for forms of public life that do not just enact a constricted "general public" or fall out into the division between "us" and "them." Moreover, because the current structure of public life induces social movements to reiterate the terms of exclusion, we seek to change not just this phantom "general public," but also those social movements that challenge the structure of the public. Thus, our critique is as concerned with those movements from "the margins," including movements for lesbian and gay rights, as it is with the mainstream. We think that these movements for social change must themselves change if they are effectively to transform the public. Tolerance is not enough. Rather, we must radically reorient our understandings and our practices of freedom, including sexual freedom.

Sex is not a luxury, but a good: a vital resource for remaking the social and saving our lives. Crucially, we cannot decide in advance what new forms of social life and ethical relation alternative sexual praxes might give rise to. The dream of this book is also the utopian dare of a robust, contestatory, and radically inclusive America—one that lives up to its promise of freedom and justice for all.

Notes

Notes to the Introduction

1. Richard L. Berke, "Flurry of Anti-Gay Remarks Has G.O.P. Fearing Backlash," *New York Times,* June 30, 1998, A1.

2. For those familiar with the influence of Foucault in our academic work, it may seem strange that we advocate freedom, given that Foucault is one of the most prominent critics of politics organized around freedom. His critique goes to the heart of modern freedom, whether it is the freedom offered by political liberalism or that envisioned by a more radical politics of liberation. At the end of the first volume of *The History of Sexuality,* for example, Foucault leaves us with only an enigmatic reference to "bodies and pleasures" and the vague possibility of "practices of freedom" that might be distinct from concepts of overarching freedom and liberation. In his later work, particularly in the third volume of *The History of Sexuality,* Foucault attempts to develop an ethics that avoids some of these liberal and liberationist problems. Our aim is to consider what it might mean to pursue practices of freedom and in so doing shift the meaning of freedom as it is invoked in public debates about sexuality. See Michel Foucault, *The History of Sexuality, Volume I: An Introduction,* trans. Robert Hurley (New York: Vintage Books, 1978), and *Volume III: The Care of the Self* (New York: Vintage Books, 1986).

3. U.S. Conference of Catholic Bishops, "A Jubilee Call for Debt Forgiveness: A Statement of the Administrative Board of the United States Catholic Conference," April 1999, and "A Good Friday Appeal to End the Death Penalty: A Statement of the Administrative Board of the United States Conference of Catholic Bishops," April 2, 1999.

4. Qtd. in Traci C. West, "The Policing of Poor Black Women's Sexual Reproduction," in *God Forbid: Religion and Sex in American Public Life,* ed. Kathleen M. Sands (New York: Oxford University Press, 2000), 138. We must also note the irony of President Clinton's public hand-wringing about the putative sexual irresponsibility of teenage girls.

5. Nancy F. Cott, *Public Vows: A History of Marriage and the Nation* (Cambridge: Harvard University Press, 2000), 198.

6. Writing for the majority that struck down Texas's criminal abortion statute, Justice Harold Blackmun asserts: "For the stage prior to approximately the end of the first trimester, the abortion decision and its effectuation must be left to the medical judgment of the pregnant woman's attending physician." *Roe v. Wade* 410 U.S. 113 (1986). Available at http://members.aol.com/abtrbng/410us113.htm.

7. *Bowers v. Hardwick* 478 U.S. 186 (1986): 186a.

8. Stephanie Coontz, *The Way We Never Were: American Families and the Nostalgia Trap* (New York: Basic Books, 1992).

9. Judith Stacey, *In The Name of the Family: Rethinking Family Values in the Postmodern Age* (Boston: Beacon Press, 1996); and *Brave New Families: Stories of Domestic Upheaval in Late-Twentieth-Century America* (Berkeley: University of California Press, 1998).

10. This assumption dates back to at least the eighteenth century, when the Scottish philosopher David Hume attempted to place religion on rational grounds. Hume thought religion was socially useful because it provided moral guidance. He also believed that by studying different religions we could locate common or shared principles and that these shared features provided an objective basis for moral decision making. The point to emphasize here is that, for Hume, religion can provide a basis for moral knowledge. Hume's views are emblematic of his own time, but they remain influential today. For a fuller discussion of these issues, especially as they pertain to the "reinvention" of religion in modernity, see Robert Baird, "Late Secularism," *Social Text* 64 (Fall 2000): 123–36.

11. See Janet R. Jakobsen, with Ann Pellegrini, "Dreaming Secularism," *Social Text* 64 (Fall 2000): 1–27.

12. See Rebecca T. Alpert, *Voices of the Religious Left: A Contemporary Sourcebook* (Philadelphia: Temple University Press, 2000).

13. Katie Geneva Cannon, *Black Womanist Ethics* (Atlanta: Scholars Press, 1988).

Notes to Chapter 1

1. In suggesting that the meaning and experience of sex have changed over time and that sexual identities are modern inventions rather than timeless categories of human life, we are here aligning ourselves with social constructionist accounts of sexuality. Such a viewpoint is buttressed by the work of many historians of sexuality, among them George Chauncy, John D'Emilio, Carolyn Dinshaw, Lisa Duggan, Michel Foucault, Estelle Freedman, David M. Halperin, Mark Jordan, Jonathon Ned Katz, Elizabeth Lapovsky Kennedy, and Jeffrey Weeks.

2. Gayle Rubin, "Thinking Sex: Notes for a Radical Theory of the Politics of Sexuality," in *The Lesbian and Gay Studies Reader,* ed. Henry Abelove, Michèle Aina Barale, and David M. Halperin (New York: Routledge, 1993 [1984]), 3–44.

3. For a full explanation of this secularization narrative and our critique of it, see Janet R. Jakobsen, with Ann Pellegrini, "Dreaming Secularism," *Social Text* 64 (Fall 2000): 1 27.

4. *Hardwick* had nothing to do with questions of forcible sodomy or coerced sex more broadly. The entire issue of sexual assault was not part of this case.

5. Michel Foucault, *The History of Sexuality, Volume I: An Introduction,* trans. Robert Hurley (New York: Vintage Books, 1978), 101.

6. Kendall Thomas, "Beyond the Privacy Principle," *Columbia Law Review* 92 (1992): 1440.

7. Thomas is here quoting Michael Hardwick's own account of the case, from *The Courage of Their Convictions,* ed. Peter Irons (New York: Free Press, 1988), 394.

8. *Bowers v. Hardwick* 478 U.S. 186 (1986): 186a.

9. Paul Morrison, *The Explanation for Everything: Essays on Sexual Subjectivity* (New York: NYU Press, 2001). David M. Halperin, *Saint Foucault: Towards a Gay Hagiography* (New York: Oxford University Press, 1995).

10. Lauren Berlant and Michael Warner, "Sex in Public," *Critical Inquiry* (Winter 1998): 547–66.

11. John Boswell, *Christianity, Social Tolerance, and Homosexuality: Gay People in Western Europe from the Beginning of the Christian Era to the Fourteenth Century* (Chicago: University of Chicago Press, 1980); Bernadette Brooten, *Love between Women: Early Christian Responses to Female Homoeroticism* (Chicago: University of Chicago Press, 1996); Mark C. Jordan, *The Invention of Sodomy in Christian Theology* (Chicago: University of Chicago Press, 1997).

12. Daniel Boyarin, *Carnal Israel: Reading Sex in Talmudic Culture* (Berkeley: University of California, 1993); Rebecca Alpert, *Like Bread on the Seder Plate: Jewish Lesbians and the Transformation of Tradition* (New York: Columbia University Press, 1997).

13. Max Weber, *The Protestant Ethic and the Spirit of Capitalism* (New York: Scribner, 1930), 36.

14. What's more, these new disciplines felt like freedom, not limitation. As Foucault has pointed out, this means that the disciplines are not exclusively or even primarily repressive, telling people what they should *not* do or who they must *not* be. Rather, the disciplines are both regulatory *and* generative, helping to shape people's experiences of themselves as particular kinds of selves with particular investments, desires, and needs. In their repressive aspect, the disciplines are enforced by the state. But in their generative turn, they are also upheld and practiced by individuals themselves, who come to internalize body regulations as their own moral law, as freedom itself. So thoroughly is this restraint naturalized that it goes unnoticed both as restraint and as specifically Reformed Protestant.

15. The Denver District Court issued a permanent injunction enjoining enforcement of the amendment, which the state then appealed. The appeal wound its way through the courts, reaching the Supreme Court in October 1995. The Court's ruling was issued in May 1996.

16. *Romer v. Evans* 116 S. Ct. 1620 (1996): 1626–27.

17. Janet E. Halley argues that the majority in *Romer* "could not have uttered this silence [around *Hardwick*] if they thought that the constitutionality of criminal statutes proscribing homosexual sodomy *a fortiori* produces the constitutionality of every species of anti-gay discrimination." Janet E. Halley, "The Status/Conduct Distinction in the 1993 Revisions to Military Anti-Gay Policy," *GLQ: A Journal of Lesbian and Gay Studies* 3:2–3 (1996): 221.

18. Janet E. Halley, *Don't: A Reader's Guide to the Military's Anti-Gay Policy* (Durham: Duke University Press, 1999).

19. See the essays gathered in *Queer Theory and the Jewish Question,* ed. Daniel Boyarin, Daniel Itzkovitz, and Ann Pellegrini (New York: Columbia University Press, forthcoming).

20. See, for example, the infamous forgery, "Protocols of the Elders of Zion," a text that "has fueled American anti-Semitism in people ranging from Henry Ford to Khalid Abdul Muhammad." Michael Rogin, *Blackface, White Noise: Jewish Immigrants in the Hollywood Melting Pot* (Berkeley: University of California Press, 1996), 69. For an extensive history and debunking of "The Protocols," see Norman Cohen, *Warrant for Genocide: The Myth of the Jewish World Conspiracy and the Protocols of the Elders of Zion* (New York: Harper and Row, 1967).

Notes to Chapter 2

1. Justin Champion, "Toleration and Citizenship in Enlightenment England: John Toland and the Naturalization of the Jews, 1714–1753," in *Toleration in Enlightenment Europe*, ed. Ole Peter Grell and Roy Porter (New York: Cambridge University Press, 2000), 133.

2. John W. Sweet, *Bodies Politic: Colonialism, Race, and the Emergence of the American North: Rhode Island, 1741–1831* (Baltimore: Johns Hopkins University Press, forthcoming).

3. Emilie Townes, *In a Blaze of Glory: Womanist Spirituality as Social Witness* (Nashville: Abingdon Press, 1995), 94.

4. Sweet, *Bodies Politic*, see especially chapter 3, "Strange Christians."

5. This line of argument was suggested to us by Barbara Johnson's beautiful reflections on the ethical import of taking words, including prepositions, seriously. Barbara Johnson, *A World of Difference* (Baltimore: Johns Hopkins University Press, 1987).

6. National Coalition of Anti-Violence Projects, "1998 Hate Crimes Report," available at www.avp.org.

7. Karen Anderson, *The Little Rock Crisis: Social Relations and Public School Desegregation, 1954–1964* (Princeton: Princeton University Press, forthcoming).

8. James Brooke, "Rocky Mountain States Resisting Move to Broaden Hate-Crime Laws," *New York Times*, February 5, 1999, A14.

9. After all, *Vanity Fair* did not send a reporter trained at the University of Wyoming into New York City to report on how racist New York was in the wake of the shooting of

Amadou Diallo, but they did send a Harvard-educated reporter to Wyoming to produce such an article about the homophobia of the west. Melanie Thernstrom, "The Crucifixion of Matthew Shepard," *Vanity Fair,* March 1999 (no. 463): 209–14, 267–75.

10. Karen Franklin, "Psychological Motivations of Hate Crime Perpetrators: Implications for Educational Interventions." Paper presented at the Annual Convention of the American Psychological Association of San Francisco, August 16, 1998.

11. Kathleen M. Blee, "Reading Racism: Women in the Modern Hate Movement," in *No Middle Ground: Women and Radical Protest,* ed. Kathleen M. Blee (New York: NYU Press, 1998), 180–98.

12. William K. Rashbaum and Al Baker, "Police Commissioner Closing Controversial Street Crime Unit," *New York Times,* April 10, 2002, B1.

13. Don Terry, "Unanswered Questions in a Fatal Police Shooting," *New York Times,* January 9, 1999, A8.

14. Johann Freedman, Letter to the Editor, *New York Times,* April 24, 1999, A18.

15. See, for example, Jodi Wilgoren, "Clique's Dark Journey Began with Black Coat," *New York Times,* April 25, 1999, A1.

16. Noel Ignatiev, *How the Irish Became White* (New York: Routledge, 1995).

Notes to Chapter 3

1. For an important discussion of the tensions between a universalizing and a minoritizing approach to gay identity, see Eve Kosofsky Sedgwick, *Epistemology of the Closet* (Berkeley: University of California Press, 1990). Janet E. Halley puts Sedgwick's universalizing-minoritizing distinction to interesting use in her analysis of the "like race" arguments for gay rights. Janet E. Halley, "'Like Race' Arguments," *What's Left of Theory? New Work on the Politics of Literary Theory,* ed. Judith Butler, John Guillory, and Kendall Thomas (New York: Routledge, 2000), 40–74.

2. Sedgwick, *Epistemology of the Closet,* 43.

3. Qtd. in *Massachusetts News,* May 24, 1999, available at www/massnews.com /doma.htm.

4. Of the fifteen sponsoring organizations, only Kerusso Ministries is explicitly an ex-gay organization. However, the fourteen other organizations have formed crucial links with the ex-gay movement, sharing both personnel and strategies. For a detailed discussion of the ex-gay movement and its organizational links to the religious right, see Surina Khan, *Calculated Compassion: How the Ex-Gay Movement Serves the Right's Attack on Democracy* (Cambridge: Political Research Associates, 1998).

5. Qtd. in Khan, *Calculated Compassion,* 12.

6. This advertisement was followed by full-page ads in *USA Today* on July 14, 1998, which featured former professional football player Reggie White, and the *Washington Post* on July 15, 1998, which featured a group of ex-gay leaders. The *USA Today* ad was placed in the sports section, presumably to capitalize on Reggie White's name recognition for that leadership. For more on this campaign, see Khan, *Calculated Compassion.*

7. In a longer version of Paulk's spiritual testimony, as part of her ex-gay ministry, she reports that the molestation in question amounted to being exposed to a teenage neighbor's pornographic magazines, which reportedly triggered an episode that "didn't involve sexual intercourse but as the boy and I played a sort of hide and seek game with the flashlight, he made sure it touched his genitals." See John and Anne Paulk, *Love Won Out: How God's Love Helped Two People Leave Homosexuality and Find Each Other* (Wheaton, Ill.: Tyndale House, 1999), 11–14. We thank Tanya Erzen, whose ethnographic study of ex-gay ministries (dissertation work in progress) helped us to place the Paulk ad in context.

8. Note the protofeminist possibilities of Paulk's narrative, possibilities raised, then quickly shut down: Paulk's response to her molestation is presented as a detour from femininity. This initial turn away from "proper" gender identity and toward "improper" sexual objects is even interpretable as a kind of feminist protest against the high costs of being a girl. From the standpoint of the ad, however, which narrates the past in the light of the present, her rejection of femininity was a defensive reaction that only layered tragedy (gender dissidence) on tragedy (sexual violation).

9. This recasting of heterosexuality and Christianity as underdogs also reminds us that what Foucault has called "reverse discourse" (in which previously marginalized groups or identities come to speak on their own behalf, appropriating the same vocabulary that has previously been used to disqualify them as subjects) is not just a strategy deployed by those on the cultural margins (as in the case of the homosexual coming-out story), but can also be used to reassert dominant values (as we have seen in Paulk's coming-out-of-homosexuality story). Michel Foucault, *The History of Sexuality, Volume I: An Introduction,* trans. Robert Hurley (New York: Vintage Books, 1978), 101.

10. That said, the ad does not leave science behind, but seeks to enlist it in the service of tolerance. The legitimating authority of science is enlisted in the fifth section of the text, which is entitled "All *leading* medical experts agree" (italics added). As Cindy Patton argues in *Inventing AIDS,* even though the American Psychiatric Association (APA) declassified homosexuality as a mental illness in 1973, that does not mean scientific models and explanations do not continue to shape the way homosexuality is talked about and argued over in U.S. public life. Cindy Patton, *Inventing AIDS* (New York: Routledge, 1991).

11. See Sedgwick, *Epistemology of the Closet;* David M. Halperin, *Saint Foucault: Towards a Gay Hagiography* (Oxford: Oxford University Press, 1995).

12. Halley, "'Like Race' Arguments"; David A. J. Richards, "Sexual Preference as a Suspect (Religious) Classification: An Alternative Perspective on the Unconstitutionality of Anti-Lesbian/Gay Initiatives," *Ohio State Law Journal* 55.3 (1994): 491–553.

13. This tailoring is on view in the Traditional Values Coalition's 1993 video *Gay Rights, Special Rights*—produced as part of the effort to repeal Cincinnati's gay rights ordinance—and is discussed at length in Janet R. Jakobsen, *Working Alliances and the Politics of Difference: Diversity and Feminist Ethics* (Bloomington: Indiana University Press, 1998). Proponents of Colorado's Amendment 2 also made targeted appeals to "minority" voters.

14. Christopher Marquis, "Military Discharges of Gays Rise, and So Do Bias Incidents," *New York Times,* March 14, 2002, A22.

15. *Rogers v. American Airlines, Inc.,* 527 F. Supp 229 (SDNY 1981).

16. Kenji Yoshino, "Covering," available at www.yale.edu/lawweb/lawfac/fiss/yoshie.pdf. For other recent discussions of *Rogers v. American Airlines, Inc.,* see Patricia M. Caldwell, "A Hairpiece: Perspectives on the Intersection of Race and Gender," *Duke Law*

Journal 2 (1991): 365–95; and Michelle L. Turner, "The Braided Uproar: A Defense of My Sister's Hair and a Contemporary Indictment of *Rogers v. American Airlines,*" *Cardozo Women's Law Journal* 7.2 (2001).

17. Rebecca T. Alpert, "Religious Liberty, Same-Sex Marriage, and the Case of Reconstructionist Judaism," in *God Forbid: Religion and Sex in American Public Life,* ed. Kathleen M. Sands (New York: Oxford University Press, 2000), 124–32.

18. Judaism offers an interesting test case for this way of thinking about religious identity, for Judaism or "Jewishness" is passed through the maternal line. However, converts to Judaism do enjoy the same status as born-Jews (although the status of conversions performed by Conservative and Reform Rabbis is a highly contested issue in Israel currently). The children of a female convert are considered Jewish. Does this make Jewishness a matter of blood, religious practice, faith commitments, or rabbinic interpretation?

19. Richards, "Sexual Preference as a Suspect (Religious) Classification," 522, n118.

Notes to Chapter 4

1. Justice Hugo L. Black, *Everson v. Board of Education,* reprinted in *Religious Liberty in the Supreme Court: The Cases That Define the Debate over Church and State,* ed. Terry Eastland (Washington, D.C.: Ethics and Public Policy Center, 1993), 64. Eastland points out that the words "at least" mean that Black is outlining "the *minimal* constitutional limitation imposed by the ban on establishment" (64n4; emphasis added).

2. For a discussion of how the provision on "charitable choice" in the 1996 Personal Responsibility and Employment Opportunity Act of 1996 along with the Bush Administration's Office of Faith-Based Initiatives enshrines in the state a specifically Protestant understanding of charity, see "Faith Based on What? A Roundtable with Rita Nakashima Brock, Mary Churchill, Mary Hunt, and Judith Plaskow," ed. Janet R. Jakobsen and Rebecca T. Alpert, *Journal of the American Academy of Religion* (forthcoming).

3. Stephen L. Carter, *The Culture of Disbelief: How American Law and Politics Trivialize Religious Devotion* (New York: Basic Books, 1993). See particularly chapter 6, "The Separation of Church and State."

4. Eastland, "Introduction," in *Religious Liberty in the Supreme Court,* 6.

5. Eastland, "Introduction," in *Religious Liberty in the Supreme* Court, 6.

6. Justice William J. Brennan, Jr., *Sherbert v. Verner,* in *Religious Liberty in the Supreme Court,* 171–72.

7. Justice William J. Brennan, Jr., *Sherbert v. Verner,* in *Religious Liberty in the Supreme Court,* 172.

8. Chief Justice Warren Burger, *Wisconsin v. Yoder,* in *Religious Liberty in the Supreme Court,* 237, 238.

9. Congress did pass a law shortly after the *Goldman* decision allowing members of the military to wear clothing with religious significance while in uniform if this clothing was "unobtrusive," but as later court cases suggest the Supreme Court continues not to recognize many claims on behalf of free exercise. Michael W. McConnell discusses *Goldman* in "What Would It Mean to Have a 'First Amendment' for Sexual Orientation?" in *Sexual Orientation and Human Rights in American Religious Discourse,* ed. Saul Olyan and Martha Nussbaum (New York: Oxford University Press, 1998), 234–60. McConnell explains the failure of the Court to recognize free exercise claims by stating that "Free exercise doctrine appears strong, but in reality is weak" (238).

10. Frederick Mark Gedicks, *The Rhetoric of Church and State: A Critical Analysis of Religion Clause Jurisprudence* (Durham: Duke University Press, 1995), 116.

11. Laurie Goodstein, *New York Times,* February 4, 2001, Week in Review, 3.

12. We consider McConnell's and Koppelman's analyses together because they both appear in *Sexual Orientation and Human Rights in American Religious Discourse.* Michael W. McConnell, "What Would It Mean to Have a 'First Amendment' for Sexual Orientation?" in *Sexual Orientation and Human Rights,* 234–60; and Andrew Koppelman, "Sexual and Religious Freedom," in *Sexual Orientation and Human Rights,* 215–33.

13. Patricia J. Williams, *The Alchemy of Race and Rights: Diary of a Law Professor* (Cambridge: Harvard University Press, 1991).

14. Koppelman says, "I remain undecided about whether I endorse this solution [the disestablishment approach]. This essay is tentative and exploratory. I have argued for in the past and remain impressed by the arguments to the effect that the state should aggressively combat the stigmatization of homosexuality" (217). McConnell, by contrast, whom President Bush nominated in 2001 to the Tenth Circuit Court of Appeals, uses the disestablishment clause to produce an argument that in many ways parallels gay neoconservative Andrew Sullivan's position (only McConnell is at points more conservative than Sullivan). Andrew Sullivan, *Virtually Normal: An Argument about Homosexuality* (New York: Vintage Books, 1995).

15. There is a rich, but largely forgotten history of feminist critique of the privileging of the specifically sexual injury of rape. For a cogent representation of these feminist arguments about the question of sexual violence, see Pamela Haag, "'Putting Your Body on the Line': The Question of Violence, Victims, and the Legacy of Second-Wave Feminism," *differences* 8.2 (Summer 1996): 23–67. See also Sharon Marcus, "Fighting Bodies, Fighting Words: A Theory and Politics of Rape Prevention," in *Feminists Theorize the Political*, ed. Judith Butler and Joan W. Scott (New York: Routledge, 1992), 385–403; Katherine M. Franke, "Putting Sex to Work," 75 *U.Denver L.Rev.* 108 (1998): 1139–80; and Ann Pellegrini, "Staging Sexual Injury: *How I Learned to Drive,*" in *Critical Theory and Performance,* ed. Janelle G. Reinelt and Joseph R. Roach (Ann Arbor: University of Michigan Press, forthcoming [second edition]).

16. Lisa Duggan, "Queering the State," *Social Text* 39 (Summer 1994): 9.

17. Gary Bauer, "Fuzzy Morality," *New York Times,* October 8, 2000, Section 4, 15.

18. David A. J. Richards, *Identity and the Case for Gay Rights: Race, Gender, Religion as Analogies* (Chicago: University of Chicago Press, 1999).

Notes to Chapter 5

1. Although we do not deny that speech can injure, we do not assume that "hate speech" (e.g., sexually harassing speech and racist and homophobic slurs) only or necessarily injures. Think here of the way in which many younger gay men and lesbians have reappropriated and reinvested the word "queer," previously a term of abuse against homosexuals. We are also wary of governmental regulations on what has come to be called "hate speech." There is a lively debate on the Left about the risks and benefits of regulating so-called "hate speech." For a discussion on the matter of injurious speech, see the essays collected in Mari J. Matsuda, Charles R. Lawrence III, Richard Delgado, and Kimberlé Williams Crenshaw, eds., *Words That Wound: Critical Race Theory, Assaultive Speech, and the First Amendment* (Boulder: Westview Press, 1993); and Judith Butler, *Excitable Speech: A Politics of the Performative* (New York: Routledge, 1997). Catharine A. MacKinnon has been a vocal advocate of regulating sexual speech (such as pornography) as conduct. See her *Only Words* (Cambridge: Harvard University Press, 1993).

2. See Bennett's address to the U.S. Naval Academy, 1997. Another version of these remarks was published in *Imprimis,* the publication of the conservative Hillsdale College. Bennett there argues that "war has always been the crucible—that is, the vessel as well as the severest test—for our core beliefs." *Imprimis* 27.4 (1998): 4.

3. For a full explanation of this view of morality, see Janet R. Jakobsen, *Working Alliances and the Politics of Difference: Diversity and Feminist Ethics* (Bloomington: Indiana University Press, 1998).

4. Eric Foner, *The Story of American Freedom* (New York: W. W. Norton, 1998), xiv.

5. Gayle Rubin, "Thinking Sex: Notes for a Radical Theory of the Politics of Sexuality," in *The Lesbian and Gay Studies Reader,* ed. Henry Abelove, Michèle Aina Barale, and David M. Halperin (New York: Routledge, 1993 [1984]), 11.

6. Carole S. Vance, "Epilogue," in *Pleasure and Danger: Exploring Female Sexual Imagery,* ed. Carole S. Vance (New York: Pandora Press, 1992 [1984]), 433.

7. Eve Kosofsky Sedgwick, *Epistemology of the Closet* (Berkeley: University of California Press, 1990), 22.

8. See U.S. Department of Health and Human Services, "Child Maltreatment 1999: Reports from the States to the National Child Abuse and Neglect Data System," chapter 3, "Perpetrators," Table 3-4 "Perpetrator Relationship to Victims by Maltreatment Type: Sexual Abuse." Available at www.acf.dhhs.gov/programs/cb/publications/cm99/index.htm.

9. For related discussions of queer world-making possibilities, see José Esteban Muñoz, *Disidentifications: Queers of Color and the Performance of Politics* (Minneapolis: University of Minnesota Press, 1999); and Elizabeth Freeman, *The Wedding Complex: Forms of Belonging in Modern American Culture* (Durham: Duke University Press, 2002).

10. Michel Foucault, "On the Genealogy of Ethics: An Overview of Work in Progress," in *The Foucault Reader,* ed. Paul Rabinow (New York: Pantheon, 1984), 350.

11. Ettelbrick and Hunter share feminist concerns with the way marriage privileges some forms of relation over others; in addition, both women also argue that marriage as it is traditionally understood and often practiced institutes gender hierarchy. Nonetheless, Hunter and Ettelbrick arrive at rather different conclusions as to the desirability of fighting for same-sex marriage. Hunter makes a feminist case for same-sex marriage. She argues that even though marriage in its present form and practice is unattractive and even oppressive to women, enlarging it to include same-sex couples could transform it in ways that would benefit all couples (straight and gay) by modeling egalitarian partnerships. Ettelbrick, by contrast, although she believes gay couples should have the right to marry, thinks that same-sex marriage diverts activist attention from larger questions of social justice. Same-sex marriage, she argues, would reaffirm a class system, in which some relationships are recognized and validated by the state (with all the benefits that come along with that recognition) and others would remain outside the fold. See Nan D. Hunter, chapters 8 and 9 in Nan D. Hunter and Lisa Duggan, *Sex Wars: Sexual Dissent and Political Culture* (New York: Routledge, 1995), 101–106, 107–22; Paula Ettelbrick, "Wedlock Alert: A Comment on Lesbian and Gay Family Recognition," *Journal of Law and Policy* 5.1 (1996): 107–66. For a queer critique of same-sex marriage, see Michael Warner, *The Trouble with Normal: Sex, Politics, and the Ethics of Queer Life* (New York: Free Press, 1999). See also Freeman, *The Wedding Complex.*

12. We ask these questions along with those other feminists and queer theorists who have taken up the project of reimagining kinship, including Kath Weston, Judith Stacey, Karen McCarthy Brown, Judith Butler, David Eng, and Elizabeth Freeman.

13. Qtd. in David M. Halperin, *Saint Foucault: Towards a Gay Hagiography* (Oxford: Oxford University Press, 1995), 81–82.

14. Foucault argues that not all norms are regulating in the same way. In order to pursue this possibility, Foucault explores the example of an ethics organized around "care of the self" in ancient Greece in contrast to modern understandings of ethics. In the first volume of his *History of Sexuality,* Foucault shows how in the modern period, ethical norms are tied to "normalization," in other words ethics is tied to the project of producing a society regulated by determinations of what is normal and what is abnormal. As a counterexample, in the third volume of *The History of Sexuality,* Foucault explores the way in which some Greek citizens took up the particular moral discipline of "aske-sis" as a means of producing a different kind of self. Foucault pursues the Greek exam-ple not to show us how ethics should be, but to make a point that is well taken and, in fact, crucial: Not all ethics are regulative in the same way. Foucault is concerned with practices of freedom not because such practices could institute a freedom from any and all norms, nor because these practices are free from power relations; rather, such prac-tices allow us to resist the modern regime in which what is "normal" is synonymous with what is "good."

15. Foucault makes these comments in relation to his exploration of the "ethics of the care of the self" in ancient Greece, an ethical system in which the ethics of the citizens who could pursue the care of the self was linked to relations of social domination. The domination to which we here refer is the direct domination of possessing—owning—others. In ancient Greece, citizens (and only [some] men could qualify as citizens) liter-ally owned both slaves and their wives. Foucault does not endorse this system, but says that he merely offers the ancient Greek case as an example of how ethics could be oth-erwise. Nonetheless, we think the problems with the Greek example are more trench-ant than Foucault acknowledges.

16. Michael Bronski, *The Pleasure Principle: Sex, Backlash, and the Struggle for Gay Freedom* (New York: St. Martin's Press, 2000), 9.

17. See, for example, Leo Bersani and Douglas Crimp, eds., *AIDS: Cultural Analysis, Cul-tural Activism* (Cambridge: MIT Press, 1988); Samuel R. Delany, *Times Square Red, Times Square Blue* (New York: NYU Press, 1999); Phillip Brian Harper, *Private Affairs: Critical Ventures in the Culture of Social Relations* (New York: NYU Press, 1999); Michael Warner, *The Trouble with Normal: Sex, Politics and the Ethics of Queer Life* (New York: Free Press, 1999).

18. Allan Bérubé, "The History of Gay Bathhouses," in *Policing Public Sex: Queer Politics and the Future of AIDS Activism,* ed. Dangerous Bedfellows (Boston: South End Press, 1996), 195.

19. Douglas Crimp, "Melancholia and Moralism," in *Loss,* ed. David L. Eng and David Kazanjian (Berkeley: University of California Press, 2002).

20. Amber Hollibaugh, "Seducing Women into a 'Lifestyle of Vaginal Fisting': Lesbian Sex Gets Virtually Dangerous," in *Policing Public Sex,* 326.

21. Elizabeth Lapovsky Kennedy and Madeline D. Davis, *Boots of Leather, Slippers of Gold: The History of a Lesbian Community* (New York: Routledge, 1993).

22. Audre Lorde, *Zami: A New Spelling of My Name* (Freedom, Calif.: Crossing Press, 1982).

23. Accusations about the amorality or immorality of queer sex, queer politics, and queer theory depend on conflating opposition to heteronormativity and all "regimes of the normal" with a rejection of all ethical norms. See Janet R. Jakobsen, "Queer Is? Queer Does? Normativity and the Problem of Resistance," *GLQ: A Journal of Lesbian and Gay Studies* 4.4 (1998): 511–36.

Index

Abortion, 3, 6, 52, 56–58, 117, 154n6

AIDS activism, 145–46

Allegheny County v. ACLU, 115,

Alpert, Rebecca, 98, 154n12, 156n12, 161n17, 161n2

American Family Association, 80

Analogies: between disestablishment of religion and sexuality, 116, 119–22; between food and sexual preferences, 137, 138; between racial and sexual justice, 16, 93, 94; between sexual and religious freedom, 16, 97, 99, 101, 103, 104–5, 106, 107, 109, 110–11, 116–17, 118–22, 125, 126, 129, 149–50

Anderson, Karen, 58, 157n7

Baird, Robert, 154n10

Bauer, Gary, 124, 163n17

Bennett, William, 131, 164n2

Berke, Richard L., 153n1

Berlant, Lauren, 28, 155n10

Bersani, Leo, 166n17

Bérubé, Allan, 145, 166n18

Birch, Elizabeth, 78–79, 89, 97

Black, J. Hugo, 104, 161n1

Blackmun, J. Harold, 34, 154n6

Blee, Kathleen, 61–62, 158n11

Boswell, John, 155n11

Bowers v. Hardwick, 15, 22–24, 38, 112, 154n7, 155n4

Boyarin, Daniel, 154n12, 156n19

Braunfeld v. Brown, 108

Bronski, Michael, 143, 166n16

Brooten, Bernadette, 155n11

Brown, Karen McCarthy, 165n12

Brown v. Board of Education, 58

Burger, J. Warren, 29–32, 40

Bush, George H. W., 71

Bush, George W., 4, 6, 103–04, 114

Butler, Judith, 158n15, 163n1, 165n12

Caldwell, Patricia M., 160n16

Cannon, Katie, 13, 154n13

Capital punishment, 5, 131

Carter, Stephen, 107, 161n3

Catholic Church, 5, 12–13, 137–38

Champion, Justin, 157n1

Chauncey, George, 155n1

Christian Coalition, 13

Christianity: as basis for law and public policy, 5, 29–32, 40, 77–78, 79, 113–14; as basis for morality, 5, 13, 14, 21, 41, 113–14, 128; as *de facto* state religion, 104, 109, 112, 113; and the religious Right, 12, 111–12. *See also* Judaism

Church-state separation, 3, 11, 14–15, 79, 107–8; as enshrined in U.S. Constitution, 107; and secularism, 11, 112, 113–14, 115. *See also* Disestablishment; *Sherbert v. Verner*; *Wisconsin v. Yoder*

Civil Rights Act of 1964, 110

Civil rights movement, 12, 59

Clinton, Bill, 6, 7, 63, 130, 153n4

Cohen, Norman, 157n20

Colorado Amendment 2. See *Romer v. Evans*

Columbine High School shootings, 4, 68, 158n15

Coontz, Stephanie, 154n8

Cott, Nancy F., 153n5

Crimp, Douglas, 146, 166n17, 166n19

Davis, Madeline D., 146–47, 167n21

Defense of Marriage Act, 63, 77

Delany, Samuel R., 166n17

D'Emilio, John, 155n1

Diallo, Amalou, 52, 63–67

Dinshaw, Carolyn, 155n1

Discrimination: against gays and lesbians, 35, 147; and analogy between race and sexuality, 15–16, 93, 94; and Colorado Amendment 2, see *Romer v. Evans*; and racial profiling, 63–64, 156n12, 156n13

Disestablishment, 103–4, 109–10, 112, 115; of sexuality, 116, 120–23, 141–42. *See also* Church-state separation; Freedom; Religion

Duggan, Lisa, 122–23, 155n1, 163n16, 165n11

Eastland, Terry, 108, 161n1

Eisenstadt v. Baird, 8

Employment Division v. Smith, 107, 108

Eng, David, 165n12

Enlightenment liberalism, 103, 124

Erzen, Tanya, 159n7

Essentialism: and appeals to "nature," 77–78, 96; vs. cultural determinism, 90; and gender, 94; and human sexuality, 20; and immutable identity, 76–77; vs. social constructionism, 154–55n1. *See also* Homosexuality

Ethics, 134, 138, 156n14. *See also* Foucault, Michel; Sex

Ettlebrick, Paula, 142, 165n11

Everson v. Board of Education, 104

Faith-based initiatives, 113, 161n2

Falwell, Rev. Jerry, 1, 76, 79, 90

First Amendment, 97–100, 103, 110, 113–15, 119, 122, 164n1

Foner, Eric, 133, 164n4

Foucault, Michel, 23, 125, 140–44, 153n2, 155n1, 155n5, 156n14, 159n9, 164n10, 165n14, 166n15

Franke, Katherine M., 163n15

Franklin, Karen, 61, 158n10

Freedom: as an American value, 8; analogy between sexual and religious, 16, 97, 99, 101, 103, 104–5, 106, 107, 109, 110–11, 116, 117, 119–122, 125, 126, 129, 149–51; as condition of equality, 105–6; and democracy, 61, 72–3, 133, 149; and everyday life, 106–7, 143; and the exercise of religion, 97–98, 104, 107–9, 110, 112, 125, 161n9; and morality, 130–33; public vs. private, 7–8, 26–27, 105–6, 107, 138

Freedman, Estelle, 155n1

Freeman, Elizabeth, 164n9, 165n11, 165n12

Gay and lesbian rights: advocacy strategies for, 16, 17, 75–76, 92–93, 96–97, 99, 100–101, 134–35; biblical arguments against, 77–78, 79, 88–89; and democracy, 39; and homophobic discourse, 88–89, 136; as "special rights," 35–36, 93. See also Freedom; Romer v. Evans

Gay Rights, Special Rights documentary, 160n13

Gedicks, Frederick Mark, 110, 112, 162n10

Georgia Supreme Court, 27–28

Gingrich, Newt, 10

Goldman v. Weinberger, 110, 162n9

Goodstein, Laurie, 113

Griswold v. Connecticut, 8

Haag, Pamela, 163n15

Halley, Janet E., 92–94, 156n17, 156n18, 158n1, 160n12

Halperin, David M., 89, 136, 155n1, 155n9, 160n11

Hardwick, Michael, 24, 27, 106

Harper, Phillip Brian, 166n17

Hate crimes, 50, 59, 61–62, 71–73, 157n8, 158n10

Heteronormativity, 28, 120, 122, 167n23

Heterosexuality, 9, 10, 26–28, 76–77, 82–84, 100, 144

Hollibaugh, Amber, 140, 167n20

Homosexuality: 9, 14, 140, 142–43; as acquired identity, 83; and analogies with race, 78, 91–92; and "born that way" arguments, 17, 76–77, 91–92, 96, 101; biblical pronouncements on, 77, 78–79; "causes" of, 91–92, 96, 98; as curable behavior, 80–83; and "ex-gay" organizations, 80–82, 159n4; as immutable characteristic, 76–77, 93; medical accounts of, 160n10; and status-conduct distinction, 36, 37–38, 75–76, 93. See also Essentialism; Sodomy laws; Tolerance

Human Rights Campaign, 84

Hume, David, 154n10

Hunter, Nan, 142, 165n11

Ignatiev, Noel, 70

Itzkovitz, Daniel, 156n19

Jakobsen, Janet R., 154n11, 155n3, 160n13, 161n2, 164n3, 167n23

Johnson, Barbara, 157n5
Jordan, Mark, C., 155n1, 155n11
Judaism, 137, 161n18; and anti-Semitism
    in *Romer*, 40–41; and false universalism
    of Judaeo-Christian morality, 31,
    100–101, 128–29; and homosexuality,
    31; and social justice movements, 12

Katz, Jonathan Ned, 155n1
Kennedy, Elizabeth Lapovsky, 146–47,
    155n1
Kennedy, J. Anthony, 35–36, 44, 167n21
Khan, Surina, 159n4, 159n5, 159n6
King, Alveda, 77, 90
Koppelman, Andrew, 116, 119–21,
    162n12, 162n14

Lesbianism, 81–84,; and sexual ethics,
    145–46
Lewinsky, Monica, 7, 130
Lieberman, Joseph, 123
Lorde, Audre, 147, 167n22
Lott, Trent, 2, 3, 82, 88
Love: as a Christian teaching, 80–81,
    82–83, 84; and model of monogamy,
    135; and sexual intimacy, 140, 146–47;
    and the sin vs. sinner distinction, 1, 13,
    36, 44, 45, 61, 94, 126; and the value of
    sex, 126
Lynch v. Donnelly, 114–115

MacKinnon, Catharine A., 164n1
Marcus, Sharon, 163n15
Marriage: benefits conferred upon,
    140–141; and definition of family, 7, 8;

as form of sexual regulation, 116, 122,
    142–43; and morality, 9–10; and pri-
    vacy rights, 7–8; same-sex, 77, 123–24,
    165n11; and welfare policy, 6
McConnell, Michael W., 116–119, 119–21,
    162n9, 162n12, 163n14
Media representation: and construction of
    the general public, 57, 63, 67–68; of
    gays and lesbians, 54–55, 68; and imag-
    ined middle America, 52–53, 55
Miller, Tyisha, 52, 64–65
Mohler, Rev. Albert Jr., 76, 79
Morrison, Paul, 155n9
Muñoz, José Esteban, 164n9
Muslims, 49, 111

National Organization for Women, 71

Patton, Cindy, 160n10
Paulk, Anne, 80–86, 88, 159n7, 159n8
Pellegrini, Ann, 154n11, 155n3, 156n19,
    163n15
Pluralism, 31, 132, 139
Powell v. State of Georgia, 27

Quakers, 12, 46

Religion: as basis for morality, 11–12,
    100–101, 128–29, 154n10; belief vs.
    practice of, 99–100, 125–26; and social
    justice movements, 12; and the history
    of tolerance, 45–47; privatization of,
    117, 120–21; in the public sphere,
    114–16. *See also* Christianity; Freedom
Republican Party, 124

Richards, David A. J., 92, 99, 125, 126, 161n19, 163n18
Roe v. Wade, 8, 154n6. *See also* Abortion
Rogers v. American Airlines, Inc., 95
Rogin, Michael, 157n20
Romer v. Evans, 15, 22, 35–44, 50, 75, 156n15
Rubin, Gayle, 20, 134, 136, 155n2, 164n5

Scalia, J Antonin, 37–44, 50, 75
Schlesinger, Dr. Laura, 1
Scott, Joan W., 163n15
Secularization, 21; history of, 33; and regulation of the body, 33
Sedgwick, Eve Kosofsky, 76, 158n1, 160n11
September 11, attacks of, 49, 111, 128
Sex: and analogy to food preferences, 137, 138; as basis for ethics and values, 16–17, 33–34, 123, 125, 126, 130, 139–40, 144–46; education in public schools, 5–6, 116; as formative of social relations, 145–47; free practice of, 123, 128–29, 141–42, 150–51; as measure of morality, 5, 130, 150–51; privatization of, 138, 143–44; in public discourse, 10, 15, 19, 139–140; regulation of, 4, 5, 10, 14, 20, 21, 25, 28–29, 37, 44, 116, 129, 133–34, 138–39, 145, 150–51; social consequences of, 129–30. *See also* Freedom; Heterosexuality; Homosexuality
Shepard, Matthew, 15, 52–56, 59–62, 76
Sherbert v. Verner, 107
Slepian, Dr. Bernard, 52, 56–57, 69, 111
Sin: and the identity-act distinction, 1, 13, 33, 40, 41, 56, 86, 116; as a theological category, 2, 71

Sodomy laws, 2, 7–9, 22–38, 43
Southern Poverty Law Center, 50
Stacey, Judith, 154n9
Sullivan, Andrew, 76, 99, 163n14
Sweet, John, 48, 157n2, 157n4

Thernstrom, Melanie, 158n9
Thomas, Kendall, 24, 155n6, 155n7
Tolerance: as agent of social hierarchy and division, 50, 68, 141; as conditional on assimilation, 16, 65–66; and democracy, 46, 148; of dissenting views, 13; vs. extremism, 58, 60, 87; history of, 45–48; and homosexuality, 14–15, 33–40, 41–42, 53, 88; and the integration of minorities, 12, 49, 65, 69–70, 73, 109; as political middle ground, 56, 58, 59, 86; and racial identity in early America, 49; and religious violence, 110; as response to hatred, 49–50, 51, 60
Townes, Emilie, 48, 157n3
Turner, Michelle L., 161n16

U.S. Constitution: and First Amendment, 97, 98, 99, 100, 103–4, 107, 116, 117, 118–19, 163–64n1; and the right to privacy, 24, 25. *See also* Discrimination; Gay and lesbian rights
U.S. Supreme Court, 3, 4, 19 22,–28, 99, 100, 109–110

Values: absolute vs. relativist, 4, 130–31; conservative rhetoric of, 133; and free exercise, 97–98, 100–101; Judaeo-Christian,

Values (*Continued*), 40–41, 128; liberal progressive, 133; and the political "center," 87, 88; and sexual practices, 16, 34, 123, 125, 126, 139, 143–47, 150–51. *See also* Christianity; Freedom; Sex
Vance, Carole, 135, 164n6

Warner, Michael, 28, 155n10, 165n11
Waterbury, Margie, 86–87
Weber, Max, 33, 156n13

Weeks, Jeffrey, 155n1
Welfare policy, 1, 5, 6, 8, 118, 161n2
West, Traci C., 153n4
Weston, Kath, 165n12
White, J. Byron, 4, 23, 25, 29, 30
White, Reggie, 159n6
White, Ryan, 51
Williams, Patricia J., 118, 162n13
Wisconsin v. Yoder, 108

Yoshino, Kenji, 95, 160n16

About the Authors

A former policy analyst and lobbyist in Washington, D.C., Janet R. Jakobsen is Director of the Center for Research on Women at Barnard College. She is the author of *Working Alliances and the Politics of Difference: Diversity and Feminist Ethics.* Ann Pellegrini is Associate Professor of Drama at the University of California, Irvine. She is the author of *Performance Anxieties: Staging Psychoanalysis, Staging Race.*

.